THE FRAGRANCE OF CHRIST

VOLUME II

FR. LOUKA SIDAROUS

STORIES OF ORDINARY PEOPLE
STRIVING FOR EXTRAORDINARY HOLINESS

The Fragrance of Christ: Volume II
By Fr. Louka Sidarous

Icons designed by: Fadi Mikhail

Translated, edited, and designed by:
St. Mary & St. Demiana Convent
330 Village Dr.
Dawsonville, GA 30534
convent.suscopts.org

Published by:
St. Mary & St. Moses Abbey Press
101 S Vista Dr.
Sandia, TX 78383
stmabbeypress.com

10 9 8 7 6 5 4 3 2 1

Introduction

In the name of the Almighty

This collection of true stories, which we have witnessed firsthand, serves as a continuation of our first book, Volume I of *The Fragrance of Christ.* That book, being well-received by both clergy and Christ-loving laypeople, had a profound impact on those who read it. The late Bishop Youannis, bishop of Al-Gharbia, who lived a life of deep love and tangible Christianity, distributed it among his priests and servants. May God grant him rest.

Similarly, the late Hegumen Fr. Youssef Asaad distributed over 5,000 copies of the book during a meeting at the Church of the Blessed Virgin Mary in El-Omraniya, Giza. The copies were a gift from one of his beloved; the Lord had delivered this man from a trial, so he asked Fr. Youssef, "What can I do, my father, to repay the Lord for His goodness?" Fr. Youssef advised him to go to St. George Church in Sporting, Alexandria, and collect as many copies of the book as he could find. At that time, the church library had 5,000 copies, and he took them all. Fr. Youssef distributed them freely to the people. Every time the book was printed, it quickly sold out, necessitating multiple reprints, totaling over 80,000 copies, all of which were distributed.

The goal of this series of small books is to nourish the spirit of faith and reliance on God. Though the trials surrounding believers increase day by day, "the Lord's hand is not shortened, That it cannot save; Nor His ear heavy, That it cannot hear" (Is 59:1). As Isaiah says, "In all their affliction He was afflicted, And the Angel of His Presence saved them" (Is 63:9). In every era, God has witnesses to truth who hold fast to His name until their last breaths. These stories do not focus on a specific group of people. They are diverse, reflecting the varied circumstances and lives of believers.

The promises of God in the Holy Gospel are true and faithful. The commandments of Christ and His words of love and compassion—whether we hear them in sermons or read them in books—are sweeter than honey (Ps 119:103). But their power lies in living them out and putting them into practice. So, let us be encouraged, my brethren, to walk the narrow path, to follow in the footsteps of our Savior, and to carry our crosses with gratitude and pride. We believe that the One who worked through the brothers and sisters whose lives are recounted in this book is able to work in us as well, enabling us to will and to act according to His good purpose for the expansion of His kingdom.

Note: We did not intend, as we wrote these words, to glorify any individuals—some of whom are still alive—or names, but rather to highlight the work of God and the power of faith in Christ, reliance on Him, and life in Him. We hope that the Lord completes our good fight, for we are all constantly striving, and the true measure of a person is always revealed in the end.

Fr. Louka Sidarous

CHAPTER ONE

Granted Understanding

Some souls accept the faith and enter the sheepfold of Christ, the Good Shepherd, when they are advanced in age. These individuals were destined for their callings before they were formed in the womb, and their selections are as clear as the sun at midday. We have witnessed this grace with our own eyes, and it brings us comfort and hope.

Christ's Church will continue to bear His spiritual children throughout the ages because the Holy Spirit, who causes the Church to bear fruit, resides in her eternally. The Church does not grow old, nor does she suffer from barrenness; rather, she remains fruitful and ever-giving. The following is just one example of someone whom grace placed in our path for encouragement and consolation. We felt it our duty to share this comfort, so that many souls may be uplifted.

A mother to both sons and daughters, this woman accepted the faith in her late 40s. When her heart opened to the Lord, it opened without hindrance or obstacle. She loved the Lord with an overwhelming, extraordinary love, and she deeply rejoiced in the cross of Christ and His precious blood.

After receiving the grace of Baptism, she became steadfast in prayer, faithfully attending the liturgies and partaking of the Holy Sacraments with an indescribable hunger and thirst.

In April 1979, I was baptizing a group of Americans at St. Mark Church in Los Angeles, California. During their procession through the church after the liturgy, while they were dressed in white and holding candles, this woman ululated loudly, overcome with joy. Her tears flowed freely as she exclaimed, "I am the only one who feels what they feel and understands the value of the grace they've received. You were baptized as children and grew up in grace, but I was deprived of it for so long. When the Lord granted me to taste the sweetness of His love, I came to truly appreciate the generosity of Christ and His abundant grace."

She would often tell me, "If envy were permitted in the Christian life, I would envy those who were born into grace, grew up in it, and enjoyed it throughout their lives."

I would respond, "Grace cannot be measured. God gives His Spirit without limit, and what one person may receive in a moment can far surpass what another has experienced over years and years."

As the Lord said, "So the last will be first, and the first last. For many are called, but few chosen" (Mt 20:16).

With her simplicity of heart and faith, this woman rejoiced in the word of God with a remarkable spiritual joy. She absorbed it with great depth, surpassing many who had been in the Church for a long time.

However, there was a significant obstacle in this lady's spiritual growth—she was illiterate. She suffered greatly because of this, as she longed to read the Bible, pray the psalms, draw from the fountain of life, and deepen her knowledge. Her only way to obtain knowledge was by listening—listening to sermons, hymns, and the readings of the Gospel. But books, to her, were sealed treasures. As she continued attending church, her yearning for knowledge grew stronger. She longed to read the word of God for herself.

One day, during the Divine Liturgy, a deacon was distributing psalms from the *Agpeya* (the Coptic Orthodox prayer book for the seven canonical hours of the day) to the congregation at the beginning of the service. He told her which one to read, but she shook her head.

This incident deeply affected her. After the liturgy, she returned home, entered her room, and cried out to the Lord with boldness, "How is it that all these people can enjoy and pray Your words, while I am deprived of this grace?" She pleaded with Him, saying, "You must grant me the gift to read."

In her anguish, she wept bitterly. And then, miraculously, she opened the *Agpeya* in her hands and found that the Lord had illuminated her mind. She began reading immediately, without a teacher, despite never having learned the alphabet.

She rushed to me, elated and filled with joy, almost flying with happiness. To my astonishment, she read the psalms fluently in my presence, without error.

She glorified the One who said—and is faithful to His promises—"None of them shall teach his neighbor, and none his brother, saying, 'Know the Lord,' for all shall know Me, from the least of them to the greatest of them" (Heb 8:11), and "they shall all be taught by God" (Jn 6:45).

CHAPTER TWO

A Chosen Vessel

The Lord's words to Ananias regarding the apostle Paul, that he is a "chosen vessel" (Acts 9:15), are truly wondrous. The Lord has kept chosen vessels in every time and place. These vessels may have once lived outside the paths prepared for them, or wandered in the world's distractions, unaware of their purpose. But when the fullness of time comes, the soul awakens to its calling, begins to walk the path of salvation, and dedicates itself wholly to the One who called it.

Among these chosen souls is a young American man from San Francisco who visited me in Los Angeles in 1979, accompanied by a dear friend. The friend said to me, "This young man has an extraordinary story of faith in Christ. I hope you'll hear it. I brought him here so he could gain more knowledge and grow in faith before receiving the sacred sacrament of Baptism."

I sat with the young man, who was tall and slender with gentle features. He began to recount his incredible story. He told me that he was Jewish and that his family was deeply religious and conservative, despite living in an area filled with temptation and sin. He was diligent in going to the synagogue every Sabbath and in observing the commandments of the Mosaic Law to the best of his ability.

He worked as a financial manager for a very wealthy woman who entrusted him with her vast riches and business affairs. He was exceedingly faithful in his work, pouring all his effort into his duties. The woman, who was in her 40s, lived a life of complete indulgence, engaging in the kind of debauchery that is common among the wealthy. The young man, then 28 years old, was deeply committed to his work. The more he demonstrated loyalty and dedication, the more she appreciated him and rewarded him generously. He was content in his work, and her admiration only fueled his commitment.

However, an unforeseen turn of events disrupted everything. The woman became infatuated with him and began to pursue him. This was something he had never imagined, and her advances filled him with a deep sense of revulsion. He tried to avoid her as much as possible, keeping himself busy and minimizing encounters with her. Her pride was wounded—how could a mere employee dare reject her? As her insistence escalated, so did his rejection, which hurt her pride even more. She then made many attempts to provoke him, which he bore quietly.

One day, her threats became explicit. She warned

him that, if he did not submit to her desires, she would take revenge on him. A few days later, he was suddenly arrested and thrown into prison. She and her lawyer had fabricated charges of embezzlement and gross negligence against him. These accusations were completely false, but she was a woman of influence and wealth.

In prison, the young man was overwhelmed with psychological pressure and a deep sense of injustice. Days passed, and he waited for the investigation to conclude, feeling completely trapped, with no refuge.

One day, an Anglican priest visited the prisoners. He spoke briefly with the young man and left him a Bible. As a devout and zealous Jew, the young man did not believe in the Bible, had never read it, and had no interest in it. Yet, in the suffocating monotony and boredom of prison, he eventually reached for the book, thinking, *What harm could it do to read it?* He opened it and began reading the account of the miraculous feeding of the multitudes, followed by the disciples' ordeal on the stormy sea, and Jesus walking on water toward them, calming the winds and waves with extraordinary authority (Mk 6:30–52).

His heart was deeply moved in a way he had never experienced before. He found himself praying an unfamiliar prayer, saying, "Lord, is this true? Is this truly Your power, Your authority over nature, and Your care for Your disciples? If You deliver me from this injustice today, I will be Your servant all my days." Within an hour, he was summoned to appear before the prosecutor general. After answering the prosecutor's detailed questions truthfully, he was immediately released without bail.

He could hardly believe his joy. His heart overflowed with the light of faith in Christ, shining like the sun at midday. A deep love for Christ welled up within him. He knelt on the ground, giving thanks to Christ, the Almighty God, for everything. He returned home rejoicing, and, as soon as he saw his neighbor, who was a Christian, he asked him to take him to a priest to be baptized. His neighbor taught him about the Orthodox faith and shared with him stories from Church history whenever he could.

The first opportunity they had, they came to me together. By then, this pure young man had read the Bible extensively and had been profoundly affected by it. I was overjoyed to meet him and had him stay with me for several days, teaching him the Old Testament, which he already knew well. But now, seeing it in the light of Christ, he understood it as a shadow and type of the heavenly realities. He was filled with indescribable joy.

Soon after, he received the grace of the Comforter, being born again through Holy Baptism. In Christ Jesus, he became a new creation, for the old things had passed away (2 Cor 5:17).

✠

CHAPTER THREE

The Word of God Is Living and Powerful

Once, while sharing stories of faith with me, Fr. Bishoy Kamel, may God repose his soul, said, "In the early 1970s, a beloved friend of mine, a civilian employee in the army, came to me accompanied by a young man in his 20s who was serving as a volunteer in the military. He introduced the young man to me. We sat together, and the young man began recounting one of the most astonishing stories of God's dealings with mankind that I had ever heard.

"He said, 'We live in a working-class neighborhood in Alexandria with no Christian neighbors. I had never interacted with a Christian before. We are a poor family; my father is a police officer, and I am the eldest of eight children. I was aggressive by nature, cruel to my siblings, and knew no mercy. This was the environment I grew up in—a household filled with shouting, cursing, and foul language. There was no peace or quiet, only an obsession with worldly songs and all kinds of impurities.

"'"One day, I was shopping, and the grocer wrapped my purchase in a scrap of paper before handing it to me. Out of curiosity, I unfolded the paper and began to read. The words struck me as strange, so I read more attentively. These words did not merely enter my mind—they pierced my heart. I realized I was reading words that had come from above—divine, heavenly, exalted words. The paper was a page from the Holy Gospel, specifically from the Gospel of Matthew, chapters 5 and 6, containing part of the Lord Jesus' Sermon on the Mount."'"

Fr. Bishoy continued, "What was astonishing—and remains beyond explanation—is that these words, which he read once and then repeatedly, transformed his character entirely. He became gentle, peaceful, compassionate toward the weak, and kind in speech, abstaining from uttering a single foul word. He even became pure in his gaze, unable to look at any woman or girl with impure intent. He felt the Gospel's miraculous power to change him. People around him noticed the transformation and were amazed. His father, thinking he was sick, asked him, 'What's wrong, son? Have you fallen ill or suffered some misfortune? You're not acting like yourself—you're unusually calm.' The young man reassured his father that he was fine.

"He became eager to learn more about the Holy Bible, longing to read it in its entirety. He approached a Christian—who would later become his spiritual guide—

and asked to borrow a Bible. He would stay up all night, reading it until dawn, never growing weary or feeling like he had read enough.

"In his confessions, he would say, 'The entire Bible is a source of joy, fulfillment, and comfort to the soul, instilling hope and leading to salvation. Yet, no matter how much I read, I always return to the Sermon on the Mount. It was my first encounter with my Savior and my first experience of Him. It was like a ray of light that illuminated my entire life. How could I forget a single word of it?'

"I bear witness before God that, the day this young man received the grace of rebirth and renewal from the Holy Spirit in the sacred waters of Baptism at the Church of St. Mark in Alexandria, his face shone like that of an angel. The moment he emerged from the baptismal font, God's grace rested upon him. The deacons I had invited to support him also attested to this. They helped him embrace the traditions, sacraments, and Christian way of life."

Indeed, "the word of God is living and powerful" (Heb 4:12).

CHAPTER FOUR

Taught by God

Fr. Bishoy Kamel also shared with me the story of another chosen soul, a woman he met at St. George Church in Sporting in the early 1970s. She would always stand in the back rows and greet the priests cautiously, with a hint of fear.

He said, "One day, I asked her, 'Are you a Christian?'

"She replied, 'No, but I love Christ deeply.'

"When she sat with me, she shared her secret. She worked for a wealthy family in Cairo and later became acquainted with a Christian man in Alexandria. This man, despite his limited understanding, would teach her about Christ and speak to her about His love. The more she learned, the more her love for the Lord and His life-giving cross grew.

"I asked her plainly, 'Does he intend to marry you?'

"She simply responded, 'Yes.'

"I said, 'My sister, Christianity is not like that. It is not a bridge to another goal. One does not become a Christian to achieve some other purpose. Faith in Christ did not spread through marriage. That is not Christianity at all. Christ is sought for His own sake, and He is loved for His cross—not for any other reason.'

"She wholeheartedly agreed, saying, 'I seek Christ for His own sake and my desire to enjoy Him and live for Him, regardless of any other matter. Whether I marry this man or not, I have tasted the grace of faith in Christ, and I will not abandon it, no matter the cost.'

"I told her, 'The only condition for you to receive the Holy Mysteries is to break your attachment to this man.'"

She agreed immediately. He entrusted her to one of the church's female servants, who cared for her, taught her the faith, and instructed her in the Gospel, the holy commandments, and the virtues of Christian life.

And so, she received the Divine Mysteries, and God's grace descended upon her. On the day of her baptism, she said, "I nearly died in the baptismal font from the overwhelming joy that flooded me. It is out of Christ's compassion and love that He does not reveal all the spiritual riches and the glory of His inheritance to the soul all at once. No one would be able to endure this. He grants us a little at a time because of the weakness of our nature and our inability to bear it."

What was remarkable about this blessed sister is that, from the moment of her baptism, it was as though she was divinely inspired, as if she knew the commandments by heart. She instinctively understood what was fitting and what was not, what was permissible and what was not. It was like she had received the very spirit of the commandments. She could discern what aligned with the Christian life and conduct without prior knowledge of what was written in the Scriptures.

She lived in our home during the holy 40 days of the Great Fast, leading a life of fasting, praying, and yearning for heavenly things that bring great joy to the heart. Whenever she read or reflected on the Holy Scriptures, her tears would flow abundantly—a testament to her deep spiritual connection with the living word of God, which is "sharper than any two-edged sword" (Heb 4:12).

CHAPTER FIVE

St. George and the Swift Deliverance

Once, the man who was serving as the janitor of the church came to me while I was baptizing a baby and told me that a woman and her mother were at the door asking to see me. I said to him, "Let them in as soon as I finish the baptism."

Afterwards, the woman and her mother entered, trembling with fear and hesitation. They greeted me cautiously, and I immediately realized that they were unfamiliar with the church. It seemed like it was the first time they had ever entered a church or met a priest. I welcomed them warmly, trying to calm them, and invited them to sit down.

I asked, "How can I help you?"

When the young woman (who looked to be about 30 years old) calmed down, she began telling me a strange story. She said, "As you can see, we are not Christians. However, we are from a religious and conservative family and live in peace with our neighbors, including a Christian family we are friends with.[1] Our Christian neighbor was kind enough to bring us here, as we are unaccustomed to entering churches. In fact, this is the first time we have ever spoken to a priest."

The young woman continued, "From my early youth, I have loved St. Thérèse.[2] I heard about her in school, and then I read her story. I was drawn to her gentleness and her patience and gratitude in enduring illness. I felt that her quiet, meek life was the most beautiful life. Somehow, she became like a friend to me—I spoke with her and loved her deeply. My connection to her grew, and I came to love everything she loved and longed to live like her.

"Years ago, a devout young man from a well-known family proposed to me. He held a respectable position, prayed faithfully at the prescribed times, fasted during the holy month, and fulfilled all the religious obligations of our faith. He was a bearded man of good character, respected by everyone. We were engaged and, eventually, married.

---

1 As this story takes place in Egypt, it is a fair assumption that this woman is Muslim.

2 St. Thérèse of Lisieux (1873–1897) is a French Catholic saint known for her "Little Way" of loving God through small, everyday acts. During her life, she endured prolonged illness with remarkable patience and gratitude, eventually dying from tuberculosis. Her autobiography, *Story of a Soul*, has inspired many with its message of joyful suffering.

"One thing I will never forget happened the day before my wedding. In a vision, I saw St. Thérèse offering me a bouquet of flowers. Oh, how happy I was! I felt an overwhelming sense of joy. Nothing on my wedding day made me happier than that gift; it was as if she was blessing my life."

I said to her, "It is beautiful that the saints in heaven feel connected to those who bond with them on earth."

She continued her story, saying, "My life was peaceful and normal, except for a recurring nightmare I had every now and then for an entire year. I would dream of a strange, terrifying, ugly figure—fierce and merciless. He would chase me, trying to attack and overpower me. I was filled with overwhelming fear. Whenever I had this nightmare, I would wake up exhausted and in a state of panic, my mind scattered. It was like I was ill, unable to gather any strength.

"My husband would ask about my condition, and I would share the details with him. Sometimes, he would try to comfort me; other times, he would mock me. We even visited religious scholars and mystics, but their words changed nothing. The reality remained the same, and my distress grew. I began to dread sleep, fearing the torment these dreams brought.

"Last night, I went to bed around 10:30 p.m. and, at midnight, the dreadful nightmare returned. The horrifying figure pursued me and, to my terror, caught me, threw me to the ground, and pinned me down. A dense darkness enveloped me—both around me and within me. I felt as though I was about to die. I could hardly breathe from the weight of fear, pain, and darkness.

"With the last remnants of my strength, as though calling from the depths of a well, I cried faintly, 'Lord, save me! Lord, deliver me!' Suddenly, I heard a loud noise—the sound of galloping hooves. The sound came closer until it reached me. I opened my eyes in fear and saw a vision of light—a man riding a horse and holding a spear in his hand. His face was beautiful and luminous, and his entire appearance was majestic. Even the horse seemed to be glowing.

"Then, the rider rebuked the darkness within me, saying, 'Come out of her!' The dark presence replied defiantly, 'No!' A fierce exchange followed, which I listened to in terror and overwhelming dread. When the shadow refused to leave, the rider thrust his spear with immense power into my chest, piercing through to my back. Instantly, as swift as lightning, the darkness vanished entirely, and a profound light, peace, and calm filled me. I awoke immediately.

"When I opened my eyes, I found my husband sitting on the bed, pale and trembling. I asked him, 'What's wrong? Are you okay?' He asked, 'Are you alright?' I replied, 'Thank God, I am fine.' Deeply moved, I sat up and shared everything that had happened with him. He dismissed it, saying, 'Calm down, and don't let your imagination get the better of you.' I tried to ask him what had awakened him or what he might have seen or heard, but he wouldn't answer.

"This morning, I woke up joyful and at peace. As I was changing my clothes, I noticed blood stains on my undergarments." She pulled out a garment from a bag she was carrying, and, indeed, there was a circular mark on both the front and back, evidence of the spear that had pierced her.

Overwhelmed with amazement, I asked her, "Do you know the great martyr St. George?"

She replied, "No."

I said, "Come with me."

I took her to the icon of the glorious martyr St. George. The moment she saw it, she cried out, "It's him! It's him!"

I sat with her and shared the story of the Prince of Martyrs while she listened intently, her face glowing with joy. I told her, "Even though you did not know St. George or call on him for help, when you cried out to God saying, 'Lord, save me! Lord, deliver me,' the Lord, blessed be His name, responded immediately. He sent one of His holy saints, who is mighty, swift to help, and able to conquer demons.

"St. George was a courageous knight on earth, renowned for his boldness and bravery. Ever since he became a martyr for Christ, his radiant horse has symbolized the power of God. The spear he wields is not physical but representative of the holy cross—the sign that terrifies demons and shatters their power."

I then taught her how to make the sign of the cross and hold fast to it. This marked the beginning of a marvelous new chapter in her life. Her spiritual life, which began as a simple friendship with St. Thérèse, was ignited by the brave Prince of Martyrs, St. George, with his mighty spear. May his prayers protect us and our children. Amen.

SAINT
GEORGE

✠

CHAPTER SIX

Peace, Peace to Those Who Are Near and to Those Who Are Far

Mazloum was a university classmate of mine in the late 1950s. Our group of friends was united by Christian love, and, during our first year at university, we decided to organize a special fellowship meeting. We chose the Church of the Blessed Virgin Mary in Rod El-Farag as our meeting place, where we would gather to pray, study the Holy Bible, and grow closer in brotherly love. This would become the first fellowship group at our university. As a group, we were bonded by our shared experiences at school and our love for the Church. These ties deepened over time.

The years passed quickly, and we all graduated, each going our separate way according to God's plan. In 1968, some migrated to America and England, while others went on mission trips to India and Russia. The majority of us remained in Cairo, Alexandria, or other major cities in Egypt, even as far as Aswan.

A few years later, Mazloum, who was working in

forensic medicine at the time, developed a chest illness. It was initially thought to be tuberculosis or a lung infection. He underwent treatment for some time until a surgeon at Qasr Al-Ainy Hospital decided he needed surgery. The surgeon scheduled the operation, and Mazloum was admitted to the hospital. On the day of the surgery, the surgeon was absent for some reason, and one of the resident doctors performed the procedure based on his own judgment. The resident doctor removed a large portion of Mazloum's lung and caused extensive damage. Mazloum emerged from the surgery in a much worse condition than before.

When the surgeon returned and saw Mazloum's state, he was furious, cursing and blaming everyone involved. After a few weeks, he decided to perform another operation to address the complications from the first surgery. This time, he removed two ribs from Mazloum's chest to create more space for the lung. However, Mazloum's condition deteriorated even further. His appearance became pitiful.

These circumstances deeply affected his four sisters (he was their only brother) and weighed heavily on the hearts of all of his loved ones and colleagues. Everyone was distressed; their only source of hope was prayer—supplications to God and to the saints for their intercessions.

The news reached his friends abroad, who were

following his condition with great concern. They were deeply saddened by his suffering. Some of them connected with each other and agreed that Mazloum should travel to London, where they hoped he would receive better treatment than he did in Egypt.

Mazloum could not afford to travel anywhere, having spent all his money on medical expenses. So, his friends abroad, who considered him a dear brother, covered his travel costs and were even willing to cover the cost of his treatment if necessary.

Mazloum departed for London from Cairo. His four sisters, their husbands, and other relatives and friends accompanied him to the airport; it was an emotional farewell.

One of his sisters, who lived in Ibrahimia, Alexandria, was particularly close to us. She was a woman of constant prayer and abundant tears. I often inquired about her brother's condition. A week after his departure, I asked her, "Have you received any news?"

She replied, "No news, no letter, no phone call."

Another week passed, and, still, there was no update.

I asked, "Do you know the address of the hospital where he was admitted?"

"No."

"Do you know the address of the friend in London

who received him?"

Again, she answered, "No."

A month passed without any word, and our anxiety grew. She would come to me with tearful eyes that never seemed to dry. We lifted up his name in the liturgies and pleaded with the Lord fervently, yet the days continued without any news.

Two more weeks passed, and, after a special liturgy we held for Mazloum, she held my hand, crying out, "Do something! I can't bear this anymore. My sisters in Cairo are in complete despair."

Overcome with emotion, I said to her, "With men it is impossible, but not with God; for with God all things are possible [Mk 10:27]."

She went straight home, entered her living room, and stood before an icon of the Virgin Mary holding the Child Jesus. She began to speak to her with intense emotion, almost as if she were confronting her. From the depths of her heart, she poured out her anguish and tears. Turning to the Virgin Mary, she cried, "Reassure me! I will not leave you until I am comforted."

She knelt in long, heartfelt prayer. Then, she rose, grabbed her Bible, and sat on the floor. She prayed, "Lord, let me hear Your voice. Reveal Your will to me." She opened the Bible randomly, and, to her astonishment, her eyes fell on this passage: "I have seen his ways, and will heal him; I will also lead him, And restore comforts to him And to his mourners. 'I create the fruit of the lips: Peace, peace to him who is far off and to him who is near,' Says the Lord, 'And I will heal him'" (Is 57:18–19).

She could hardly believe her eyes. Did she truly read those words? Her heart leaped with joy. She was filled with faith and peace, and she knelt again, offering heartfelt thanks to God. How could she ever repay Him for such comfort?

Filled with confidence, she called her sisters to share the news. They asked, "Did you receive a letter or hear anything reassuring?"

She replied, "No, but I received something far greater—a promise that is reassuring beyond measure."

Indeed, the Lord worked wonders for us. The next day, she received a reassuring letter. After that, good news continued to flow day by day. Within a few months, Mazloum returned from London in good health. He felt God's hand at work in his life every day, as he was being sustained by the strong faith and many prayers of his loved ones.

Truly, how great is the goodness of the Lord, and how faithful are His promises!

✠

CHAPTER SEVEN

St. Mark the Evangelist

In March 1967, we were gathered around His Holiness Pope Kyrillos VI at the Monastery of St. Mina the Wonderworker in Alexandria. It was a Sunday during the Holy Great Fast, and the pope had just finished praying evening Vespers. As the patriarch exited the church, some of the brothers surrounded him, asking about the intercessions of the saints. The discussion turned to St. Mina the Wonderworker, St. George the Great Martyr, and St. Mark the Evangelist, who aid believers through miracles.

The pope remarked, "Our own sins are what hinder their work, for they intercede for us constantly."

I asked him, "How is that so?"

He turned to me and said, "Pope Kyrillos V would spend long hours in his cell at the Patriarchate in Alexandria. There was a gardener employed to tend the garden of St. Mark Cathedral. This gardener was a devout man, deeply prayerful, who would stay up late watering the plants. This man's spiritual eyes were open, and he would see divine visions. Every night, he would see St. Mark walking around the entire area with a censer filled with incense. The man was filled with indescribable joy because of this divine blessing. No one else knew anything about it.

"One night, the gardener did not see St. Mark as he usually did. He prayed and sang hymns to God, but the vision of St. Mark did not appear the next night or the night after. Troubled and heartbroken, the man didn't know what to do. He decided to go to the patriarch's cell and share what had happened, asking, 'What could this mean?' The pope told him, 'Pray, my son, and God will reveal the matter.'

"The pope then inquired about the state of St. Mark Cathedral and its servants and discovered that the two priests serving at the church had quarreled a few days earlier and were not on speaking terms. The pope summoned the two priests, reconciled them, and sent them away in peace.

"The next day, the pope asked the gardener, 'How are things now?' The man fell at the pope's feet in gratitude, saying, 'Thank God, Your Holiness, St. Mark has returned as before.'"

Pope Kyrillos VI then said, "You see, my son, how our deeds can hinder the blessings meant for us?"

CHAPTER EIGHT

The Guardian Angel

The Church of Archangel Michael in Qafr Al-Nahal is located near cemeteries in a poor area and is mostly surrounded by non-Christian households. Since its establishment, the church has faced various attacks, including arson and destruction, but it has always been guarded by God's care.

In 1946, a simple monk was serving at the church, which, at that time, was a small building surrounded by a wall with a locked gate made of iron bars. This monk was deeply reliant on God and carried out his ministry by visiting families and celebrating the Sunday liturgies. He faithfully fulfilled his service using the limited resources available to him.

One evening, the monk was visiting a devout family. The husband was a well-off man, and his wife was a pious woman. After many years of childlessness, God had blessed them with a son, whom they cherished as the light of their lives. These new parents gave thanks to God for His kindness.

As they sat with the monk and discussed God's works

and the miracles of His saints, their 1-year-old son, who was crawling around the room, reached up to the table, on which a small bowl of lupini beans had been placed. In a brief moment of the parents' inattention, the child grabbed a bean and put it in his mouth. He tried to chew but couldn't and ended up swallowing it, so it became lodged in his windpipe. Without warning, the child collapsed, coughing violently and struggling to breathe.

The parents screamed in terror, while the monk stood paralyzed, not knowing what to do. Hoping to save the child, he decided to rush to the church to get some *Laqan* water or oil from the *qandeel*.[3] He ran quickly to the church, which was only a few minutes away, but found it locked with no one inside. The church caretaker had left and was nowhere to be found.

Desperate, the monk reached through the iron bars of the gate and grabbed a handful of soil from the church grounds. Holding it tightly, he ran back to the house, where a crowd of neighbors had gathered, drawn

3 The *Laqan* (لقان), literally meaning "basin" in Arabic, colloquially refers to the water blessed during the Liturgy of the Blessing of the Water. In this liturgy, the priest prays over the water and washes the feet of the congregation in prayer, following Christ's example (Jn 13:3–5). A portion of this blessed water is then set aside and preserved for the blessing of the people. The *qandeel* (قنديل), meaning "lamp" in Arabic, is colloquially used to refer to the oil-filled lamp lit in front of icons in many churches, as well as the lamp that holds the oil that is prayed over during the sacrament of the Unction of the Sick.

by the parents' cries. Resources in this poor area were scarce; no one could offer more than tears.

The child's condition had worsened. His face had turned blue, and he was barely breathing. The monk, breathless and clutching the church soil, rushed to the child. He uncovered the child's chest, made the sign of the cross with the soil, and cried out to God, interceding through the great Archangel Michael. Suddenly, the child sneezed repeatedly, expelling fragments of the lupini bean. He began breathing normally again.

Everyone present was astonished by the miracle, praising God and saying, "Even the soil of the church is blessed and works wonders through the Lord."

This was not the only miracle associated with that church—wondrous incidents continued to occur there. In 1948, a group of non-believers attacked it, burning some pews and attempting to destroy the interior. However, the Lord glorified His church that day. One of the attackers, holding an axe, climbed atop the altar screen but fell and struck his head, splitting it open. Seeing this, the others, who were throwing fireballs at the church, fled in fear. The church was miraculously saved, for Archangel Michael was guarding it.

There was another event involving the young daughter of a deacon. One evening, the girl's mother sent her to fetch her father, who had stayed late with other deacons practicing hymns at the church. As the 6-year-old approached the church, she saw Archangel Michael in a majestic form. He appeared as a towering figure standing at the church gate, his legs as tall as the iron gate, with wings stretching over the church and its domes.

Terrified, the girl screamed. The archangel bent down, comforting her, and gently said, "My dear, do not be afraid. What do you need?"

She stammered, "I'm looking for my father."

He replied, "Your father was here with the deacons. They have finished their hymns and left."

The girl asked innocently, "What are you doing here?"

He answered, "I am the guardian of the church."

"What is your name?"

"I am Michael."

Thus, the mighty Archangel Michael has always been a protector and guardian of this church. According to the teachings of the fathers, Archangel Michael is the guardian of every church. For this reason, a church in the name of Archangel Michael is built in the center of every monastery as a testament to the power of his intercessions and protection.

ARCHANGEL
MICHAEL

CHAPTER NINE

Hail to St. Mina the Wonderworker

Amm Aziz was a simple man who loved Christ with a pure heart. He owned a car repair shop in Alexandria. Among the priests in that area, only Fr. Bishoy Kamel and Fr. Mina Iskander had cars to use for their ministry, and Amm Aziz was always delighted to service their vehicles. He repaired them faithfully, prioritizing their needs over all other work, and he never accepted payment, not even for spare parts, despite their insistence. And so, the Lord's blessings filled his home and his whole life.

Amm Aziz attended liturgies and partook of the Holy Eucharist regularly, and he lived out his Christian faith with simplicity in his work and his interactions with others. He often asked the priests to connect him with poor families, so he could train their children. He would mentor young boys, teaching them the mechanics trade. His goal was to help them learn a skill that would benefit both themselves and their struggling families. Indeed, these boys found in Amm Aziz a father and a teacher.

While teaching them car mechanics, he also passed on the Christian life and its values. In those days, the culture of workshops often involved rough language, cheating, lying, and unwholesome behavior, which deterred many Coptic families from sending their children to learn trades. Amm Aziz's workshop thus became a haven for these vulnerable young people, bringing blessings to many families.

Amm Aziz was beloved by the late Pope Kyrillos VI. As soon as the pope would arrive in Alexandria, Amm Aziz would visit him and obtain the apostolic blessing. He would also inspect the pope's car, which was the same car left by the late Pope Yousab II. Pope Kyrillos VI did not wish to replace it, despite its many mechanical problems.

Amm Aziz also repaired the tractors and trucks that belonged to the Monastery of St. Mina the Wonderworker. He visited the monastery frequently to obtain St. Mina's blessing and joyfully help with repairs.

He was, therefore, deeply attached to the great martyr St. Mina. Indeed, he had a strong love for all the saints, whose names he repeated all day as he worked. If you met him at any hour of the day, regardless of how busy he was or how much was being asked of him, you would always find him joyfully smiling and enjoying profound peace with God.

Because of his faith, Amm Aziz's language was free of the derogatory expressions common to workshop environments. He treated everyone kindly, calling them "my son," "my dear," "my child," or "my father," and always expressed gratitude and humility in his interactions.

His example refutes the excuse of "occupational sins" or "sins of the trade," where people blame their jobs for their moral lapses. Remarkably, the boys mentored by Amm Aziz adopted his values and language when they later became business owners themselves. The Christian life and the life of pleasing God is not just taught—it is handed down from generation to generation.

A Trial

Life is not without trials. As it is written, "Yet man is born to trouble, As the sparks fly upward" (Job 5:7). While trials are a universal part of human life, for God's children, they refine faith, cultivate patience, and kindle hope. When patience completes its work, as the apostle says, one becomes "perfect and complete, lacking nothing" (Jas 1:4).

So, trouble began in the life of Amm Aziz. His eldest son, a devout and courteous university student, experienced a severe psychological illness that nearly drove him to madness.

Amm Aziz's only refuge was God. He prayed with

his whole heart and sought the intercessions of the saints. While working, he would pray silently, often weeping without anyone noticing. Despite his anguish, he remained a man of prayer who trusted in the Lord.

A Visit to the Monasteries of St. Macarius and St. Pishoy

One day, I visited Amm Aziz to check on him and his son. He told me that his son's condition was worsening but added, "I have hope in Christ, and I hold fast to His saints."

He then asked me to accompany him and his son the next day to the Monastery of St. Pishoy in Wadi El-Natrun because he had heard about Fr. Pemwah, a monk there, and believed that, through this monk's prayers, God would cure his son. He also wanted to go to the Monastery of St. Macarius the Great, near the Monastery of St. Pishoy, to receive the blessings of the three saints Abba Macarii and the 49 Martyrs of Scetis. I wanted to honor Amm Aziz's many acts of kindness toward us and the church, so I gladly accepted his request. We agreed on a time, and, the next morning, we set out early in his car. My wife and my son, Arsani, also accompanied us. During the drive, we prayed the first hour psalms of the *Agpeya* and then talked about God's works and the miracles of His saints. Immersed in prayer and holy conversation, we temporarily forgot about the boy's illness and psychological burden.

As we approached kilometer 30 on the road from Alexandria to Cairo, near the turnoff to the Monastery of St. Mina, I suggested, "Let's take this road and visit St. Mina the Wonderworker." Amm Aziz hesitated, saying, "Please, Father, don't suggest that. My heart is set on visiting the Monasteries of St. Macarius and St. Pishoy, and my son is eager to go as well. I also have a history and many stories with St. Mina."

Curious, I asked, "What do you mean?"

He explained, "On many Sundays, I'd plan to visit other churches, but whenever I passed by St. Mina's Church, something happened—a flat tire, a broken axle—forcing me to stop. I'd end up praying at St. Mina's Church. So please, don't say that. Let us go on and complete our journey in peace."

We laughed and continued on our way. However, just five or six kilometers later, Amm Aziz suddenly exclaimed, "What did I tell you, Father? What should I do now?"

He stopped the car abruptly. Alarmed, we asked, "What happened?"

He replied, "St. Mina did it again, Father!"

I asked, "How, dear Aziz?"

"The oil meter indicator has gone down to zero."

"What does that mean?"

"It means the engine's oil circulation has stopped, and, if we continue driving, the engine will burn out."

"What is the solution, then?" I asked, shocked.

"The only solution is to have the car towed back to Alexandria."

"Can we drive slowly?"

"That is impossible, Father."

"Can we repair the car here? Do you have the tools?"

"The engine would need to be completely disassembled, and this is only possible at the shop. The work would take two full days."

He stepped out of the car, hoping to find a passing truck willing to tow us back to Alexandria.

Seeing his distress, I suggested, "Why not return to St. Mina's Monastery? Let's reconcile with St. Mina, offer praises, and seek his intercession."

We began the veneration praises, and Arsani used small cymbals as an accompaniment. Then, when we sang "*Axios*" ("Worthy") to St. Mina, I said to Aziz, "Start the engine."

He turned the key, and, to everyone's amazement, the oil gauge returned to normal, and the engine worked perfectly.

I said, "Let us go back on the road to St. Mina."

So, we turned back towards Alexandria, heading to the Monastery of St. Mina. Three or four kilometers later, I asked how things were, and Aziz, who was skillful and knew his car perfectly, said everything was going well.

When he was sure about the car, he reconsidered, saying, "I do not want to disappoint my son. Let us go back to the Monastery of St. Pishoy, for fear that my son's psychological condition will get worse."

I said, "As you wish, since you said there is no problem with the car."

So, he made a U-turn, and we returned to our original route.

As soon as the car began to head toward Cairo, Amm Aziz exclaimed again, pointing to the oil gauge, "Look! Look!"

I glanced and saw the gauge rapidly dropping to zero. He immediately slowed down and stopped at the side of the road.

I said, "Amm Aziz, everything was working fine just moments ago. Why did you go back?"

He replied, "What should we do now?"

I said to everyone in the car, "Sing *'Axios'* to St. Mina the Wonderworker."

We all sang, and I said to Aziz, "Now, begin driving."

Once more, everything seemed to be in good condition. We went back on the road to St. Mina, as though nothing had happened.

This miraculous event happened three times in total that day, leaving us in awe. It was as if St. Mina was personally controlling the car's oil circulation. When the car headed toward his monastery, everything functioned normally; when it turned away, the oil circulation would stop completely. I say to the reader that, if I had not witnessed this incident with my own eyes, I truly would have considered this story an exaggeration. Yet, we were four adults and a young child, and we all saw it happen.

Eventually, as he had no choice, Amm Aziz submitted to the strange joke of St. Mina and his insistence on blessing us in his monastery that day. We went back on that road and arrived in about 50 minutes. We had to stop about 200 meters from the monastery because our car got stuck in a pool of mud, as the road was not paved. We had to push the car, and our clothes became covered with the dust of St. Mina, which heals illnesses.

Finally, we reached the monastery to pray the liturgy. Later that day, Fr. Mina Ava Mina, the steward of the monastery, laughed and said, "Why didn't you come willingly? Must we force you?"

We all left with a renewed sense of the saints' joy

when we visit their sacred places and their eagerness to support us when we are weak.

Indeed, I had not visited that monastery for a long time. I truly felt that the saints rejoice when their beloved friends are in their residences. This is like the joy of a hospitable person when he receives guests. The saints are particularly happy to support our weakness with prayer, so that we can complete our mission and repentance, bringing joy to heaven.

We returned home at the end of the day, marveling at the miraculous events and the saints' love and extraordinary power. As we were driving back, my eyes frequently glanced at the oil gauge, which remained steady at the optimal level, with everything functioning perfectly.

This car remained with Amm Aziz for more than a year after that, and, whenever I asked him about it, he would recall the events with wonder. "I've never experienced anything like that in my life," he would say. "It strengthened my faith and made me realize that the saints are not only alive in heaven but also near us on earth, feeling our struggles and supporting us in our weaknesses."

Whenever Amm Aziz and I met, he often said to me, "Believe me, Father, I love Christ very much with all my heart—a pure love unlike any other. But I am a sinner.

Tell me, what should I do to repent and become a better Christian?"

Once, he shared a dream with me: "After Pope Kyrillos' departure, he gave me the holy Blood of Christ three times in a dream! Why did he do that, Father? I am a sinner, and I am not worthy."

I felt that this kind man had a pure heart, and so, I said to him, "'Blessed are the pure in heart, For they shall see God' [Mt 5:8]."

This shows how this simple man lived close to the heart of the saints. They were in his mind and heart, and he always talked about God's deeds through His saints. When he finished his race, he departed to the Lord, leaving behind a good name and legacy.

ⲠⲒⲀⲄⲒⲞⲤ
ⲀⲂⲂⲀ
ⲘⲒⲚⲀ

CHAPTER TEN

Om Murad, Friend of the Angels

Om Murad was a pious woman who lived among us for many years, and we knew her well.[4] Truly, she was a beautiful icon of the sweetness of life with God. She had both the simplicity of a small child and the profound faith of someone who deeply trusted the Lord.

God had blessed her with an extraordinary familiarity with the saints, particularly Archangel Michael, to whom she had been deeply connected since her youth. Her faith and experience of his intercessions continued to grow over the years as the events of her life unfolded. She had an unshakable belief that, if she requested his help, her petitions would undoubtedly be granted, no matter how impossible they seemed.

4 *Om* (أم) is an Arabic word meaning "mother" that, when followed by the name of a woman's eldest son (as is the case here), is used as a respectful title expressing endearment and honor.

A Remarkable Encounter

One day, Fr. Bishoy Kamel and I were celebrating the Divine Liturgy at our beloved St. George Church in Sporting. It was around 1969. After the liturgy, this woman approached me. She was simple in her outward appearance. She told me she was a widow and the mother of three young men and that, before her husband passed away, she had lived in Beni Suef. She sat with me and spoke about her desire to build a church in the name of the great Archangel Michael.

Honestly, I did not take her words seriously at first because she was a poor woman, and building a church requires significant funds—not to mention the many obstacles that would have to be overcome. As I listened to her politely, she pulled out a bundle of cloth tied in a knot and handed it to me, saying, "Take these 50 pounds and build a church in the name of the archangel."

I replied, "Dear lady, 50 pounds isn't even enough to buy the marble for the altar. We are currently building a church in Ibrahimia in the name of St. Takla Haymanot, who is a friend of Archangel Michael. Perhaps we could use this money to build an altar in that church in the name of Archangel Michael. This would fulfill your purpose, but building an entire church is impossible."

My words seemed to unsettle the woman. She took back the bundle of money, saying, "Give it back—don't you have faith?"

I asked her, "Faith in what?"

She replied, "Faith that God can work through the little."

She then began recounting the wonders Archangel Michael had performed for her, concluding with, "Ask for something from heaven—trust me, it will come to you. Don't doubt it! The archangel has done countless miracles for me. Keep the money, and, when the church is built, let this money be the leaven for blessing. The church will be built. I have never asked for anything and not received it."

I was amazed by this woman and went to Fr. Bishoy to tell him about her story. He said, "Let it be according to her faith. Keep this deposit, and let us wait to see what God does."

And so it was. Within a week, a respectable man, over 60 years old, came to the church with his wife. We had no prior acquaintance with this man, but he asked to meet with us. It happened that Fr. Bishoy and I were both at church at the time.

When the man sat down, he introduced himself as Mr. Mikhail, an English language instructor. He and his wife had no children and lived in a villa they owned in the Mustafa Pasha area. He said he wanted to donate this villa to the church because he had no heirs and did not wish to hold on to earthly possessions.

Fr. Bishoy asked him, "What should we do with the villa?"

Mr. Mikhail replied, "Turn it into a church."

Fr. Bishoy responded, "Let us pray and seek God's guidance in this matter."

A few days later, we visited Mr. Mikhail at his villa. It was small and located on a narrow, unlit street in a remote area, with little surrounding activity. It was a desolate area, not heavily populated, with only a few Christians. We wondered if it could even serve as a church. We prayed and placed the matter before God. At that time, Pope Kyrillos VI was in Alexandria, so we went to him and presented the situation. The pope said, "Tomorrow, things will change. It will become a good church. Go and have him make the transfer of ownership."

The next day, Mr. Mikhail signed the property transfer at the Patriarchate, declaring that he was relinquishing ownership of the villa to the Patriarchate for the establishment of a church in the name of Archangel Michael. In the event the church was not built, ownership would revert back to him.

That same day, Fr. Bishoy asked me, "Where is the 50 pounds from the woman devoted to Archangel Michael?" I brought it, and we gave it to the contractor to begin working on demolishing the villa and constructing a simple building for the Church of Archangel Michael in Mustafa Pasha.

While the workers were digging up the foundation, they discovered a piece of limestone engraved with a *qurban* design filled with crosses.[5] This left no doubt in our minds that this work had been divine from the very beginning. I immediately realized that the widow's desire to build a church was inspired by an unseen hand. God was moving the hearts of His chosen ones to fulfill His will.

Charity in Many Places

Later, I learned that Om Murad would travel annually to distant places in various dioceses—villages, settlements, and rural areas that no one knew about. She performed acts of mercy for churches and poor people, as much as her limited circumstances allowed and often beyond her means. She would visit villages in Faiyum, Beni Suef, and, occasionally, Aswan.

As the years passed and she could no longer endure the difficulties of travel, she began sending aid to these distant places. She would rejoice immensely when she

5 *Qurban* (قربان), Arabic for "offering," refers to the bread prepared for Holy Communion. One loaf is chosen to become the Body of Christ through the Holy Spirit. It bears a seal with a central cross, 12 smaller crosses, and the chant of the Trisagion ("Holy God, Holy Mighty, Holy Immortal") written in Coptic letters.

heard about places of worship in these areas, and she would encourage the local communities. Occasionally, she would ask me for altar coverings or liturgical vessels to send to them. She was truly wonderful, as God had placed great love and a passion for service in her heart.

From Where Does My Help Come?

One day, she was sitting on the balcony of her home. The Feast of Archangel Michael (12 *Paone* in the Coptic calendar) was approaching. Her heart yearned to give alms, visit the sick, and help the needy, but her resources were very limited. When her husband passed away, he left her with three sons and only a modest pension. Her financial situation left her with nothing to offer. So, she prayed, lifting her eyes to heaven, and even reproached the archangel, saying, "Why have you left me in this state, where I have nothing to give?"

Suddenly, the archangel appeared to her in a glorious vision, comforting her. She remained seated in awe. Shortly afterward, she went back inside, and the postman knocked on her door to deliver a letter. Inside was a check from the pension office for overdue payments. She thanked God profusely, and her faith grew even stronger.

Within two days, she was on her way to Beni Suef, Faiyum, and the places she had regularly visited to carry out her acts of mercy and serve the brethren of the Lord.

In Place of the Housemaid

The Lord blessed her with the graduation of her eldest son, Murad, from engineering school. Murad then hired a housemaid to help her, paying the maid 2 pounds a month. However, given her limited financial resources and her belief that she could manage the household chores on her own, Om Murad decided to dismiss the housemaid. She said to me, "I'll do the housemaid's work myself, and I can distribute her salary to others in need."

Later that day, she confided in me, saying, "My conscience is troubled because I let her go. I truly hope she can find another source of income, but I don't mind the hard work—God helps me so that I can help His children."

My Strength Is Made Perfect in Weakness

One day, Om Murad began experiencing severe fatigue and an intense headache that no remedy could relieve. After a few days, her children insisted that she see a doctor. Reluctantly, she finally gave in to their pressure and, the next day, went to the clinic of Dr. Aziz Zaki, a doctor of internal medicine at El-Raml Station in Alexandria.

She was so exhausted she could barely keep her eyes open while waiting to see the doctor. When her turn came, she entered the examination room. Dr. Aziz Zaki was alarmed—her blood pressure was dangerously high. He feared for her life.

He asked, "Who came with you?"

She replied, "No one."

"That's impossible! You can't go home alone!"

She lived on Khaled Ibn Al-Waleed Street in Sidi Beshr, which is far from El-Raml Station. The doctor handed her a prescription and said, "Get this filled immediately, grab a taxi, and go home at once. In fact, you should be admitted to the hospital."

She thanked him and said, "Doctor, by the grace of Christ and the intercessions of Archangel Michael, I'll be fine."

When she left the clinic, she neither bought the medication nor took a taxi. Instead, she went to the Church of St. Mark the Evangelist. Standing before the icon of Archangel Michael, she prayed, weeping.

She was in perfect health when she left the church, as if she had never been ill. She returned home, glorifying God.

Later that day, when her son, who was in his final year of medical school, returned home, she said to him, "My son, measure my blood pressure." He did, and it was completely normal. She recounted the doctor's warning, and the family glorified God, offering a hymn of praise to the leader of the heavenly hosts.

Archangel Raphael

In 1984, Om Murad came to me, radiant with joy at the Lord's work in her life—how He had blessed her children and granted them the desires of their hearts; Murad was a successful engineer, and her second eldest was a young doctor.

One of God's latest miracles for her involved her second-oldest son, who wished to work for some time in Saudi Arabia. He had applied for a role at a hospital there, but, after an interview with a Saudi delegation, he found the conditions unsuitable and did not proceed. A year passed, and the same delegation returned to Egypt to conduct interviews with doctors. He met with them again, this time presenting his own terms regarding salary and other matters. However, the delegation did not agree to his conditions, and he returned from Cairo visibly disappointed. When his mother asked him what happened, he recounted the details of the meeting, saying that they had rejected his terms, so he left, feeling defeated. It happened to be the eve of the Commemoration of Archangel Raphael (2 *Nasi*), so this righteous mother lifted her heart in prayer, saying, "Oh Archangel Raphael, joyful comforter, if you bring joy to my son's heart and lift this sorrow from him, I will bring joy to your heart by building a church in your name." In her bold faith, she added a condition, saying, "If you send joyful news to my son before midnight, I will know that the Lord has heard my prayer through your accepted intercession." Amazingly, just a few minutes before midnight, the house phone rang; it was the head of the Saudi delegation, informing her son that all his conditions were accepted and that he had been granted the job.

After telling me this story, she said, "I will bring you a large donation this time to build a church in honor of Archangel Raphael, who has truly gladdened my son's heart. He is indeed the giver of joy."

By divine providence, at that very time, we had been searching for a piece of land to establish a new church in an area where one was needed, but we had not yet been successful. When we met with this pious mother, we saw it as a sign from the Lord and rejoiced. That day, as she joked with Fr. Kyrillos Dawood and some servants, she said, "The last time, the amount was 50 pounds, but this time, it will be 200 pounds!"

And sure enough, a few days later, she brought an envelope containing exactly 200 pounds. I kept it as a blessing, sensing it was a small leaven capable of fermenting the whole dough (Gal 5:9). Within a few weeks, we had purchased a plot of land for 200,000 pounds, where a church was built in honor of Archangel

Raphael, the joyful comforter.

St. Macarius the Great

Murad worked as an engineer at a company called *Awlad Makar* ("Makar's Sons"). His worksite was located along a desert road near the Monastery of St. Macarius the Great in Wadi El-Natrun. Because of the distance, he would often stay at the site for a week or more, returning to Alexandria for a day or two before going back to work.

Whenever he had time, he would visit the Monastery of St. Macarius to receive blessings and hear a beneficial and comforting word from the fathers, the monks. As his relationship with the fathers deepened, he would assist in repairing the monastery's heavy equipment and cranes, as this was his area of expertise.

When he returned home for his weekly leave, he would share stories of his time at the monastery and his interactions with the monks. His mother would pray for his well-being. Her heart was burdened by the fact that he lived so far away; she often prayed that he might find work closer to her, in Alexandria.

One day, while her heart was preoccupied with this thought, she lifted her kind heart in prayer, and St. Macarius appeared to her, though she had never heard of him and knew nothing about him. He spoke with her, and she realized that it was his monastery that Murad had been serving, so she pleaded with unwavering faith that he transfer Murad's work from the desert to Alexandria. She said, "It's enough—he has spent enough time living near you, serving your monastery and repairing the monastery's equipment." That same week, Murad was transferred to the company's headquarters in Alexandria.

She later described the saint to me as an elderly man with a very dignified appearance, tall and slender. Her description precisely matched historical accounts of him.

Such was the life of this blessed mother—a life marked by a series of wonders and miracles. The hand of the Lord, which sustained her, especially through the intercessions of Archangel Michael, was evident to everyone around her. Archangel Michael never failed to fulfill her requests, and he accompanied her until she departed in peace to the Lord.

ⲠⲒⲀⲢⲬⲎ
ⲀⲄⲄ
ⲢⲪⲖ

✠

CHAPTER ELEVEN

Victory Over Death

In the early days of our time at El-Marg Prison in September 1981, the atmosphere was laden with uncertainty and darkness.[6] No one anticipated what had happened, and no one truly understood what was going on. It felt as though the darkness had engulfed us from every side, but our hope in Christ remained the only ray of light. The reverend fathers who were imprisoned came from all over Egypt, and many of them did not know each other. Those early days passed very slowly and were very heavy on our souls.

Every morning, we awoke to the sound of a priest's voice, a voice filled with comfort, as he prayed sections of the Divine Liturgy. His voice carried a spiritual melody that lifted the weight of sorrow imposed by the prison and its guards.

This priest was from El-Maragha, Sohag. As the

---

6 In September 1981, amid political tensions, President Anwar Sadat of Egypt ordered the incarceration of numerous religious figures, including Fr. Louka, who was confined in Wadi El-Natrun and El-Marg prisons, along with several other clergy members.

days passed, his prayers became like the crowing of the rooster at dawn, heralding the dispersion of darkness. My cell was situated in the middle of the wing, which had three sides. This priest's cell was at the far end of the first side, so there was no opportunity to meet with him. The wing's only bathroom was near my cell, so I would only see him when it was his turn to bathe. As he passed by, I would watch him through the small opening in my cell, no larger than a clenched fist. He would greet me, though he didn't know who I was.

Due to his chest allergy, he was allowed to bathe daily. Even in the bathroom, he continued to pray, offering intercessions for the peace of the Church and for the fathers. As I listened closely to his prayers, I heard him say, "The president, the soldiers, and the officers… grant them rest, O Lord." None of the officers or guards understood what he was saying. Some of the fathers would respond with, "Amen."

Before long, the Lord worked His wonderful deeds and answered our prayers. We were transferred to a prison in Wadi El-Natrun, where we all lived together in a single ward for several months, becoming closely acquainted. When I got to know this priest better, I discovered that he was a deeply sensitive, simple-hearted man. He had nine children and was full of emotion, often moved to tears. He also had many moments of joy, smiling and laughing warmly. His simplicity of heart was reflected in his relationship with Christ, which was free of anxiety or complication. He loved the Lord with the purity of a child.

Our bond grew strong. As we walked together, we spoke of God's works, meditated on His promises, and discussed the lives of the saints. He would often shed tears during these conversations.

He once told me about one of the most astonishing events he had ever experienced during his service. It happened on Bright Saturday.[7]

After staying up all night in church for the service, which ended at 7 a.m. with the conclusion of the Divine Liturgy, he returned home to rest. Not long after, he was woken up in alarm with the words, "Get up—there's a funeral!"

Startled, he rose from his deep sleep and asked, "Who died?"

They replied with the boy's name, saying he was only 13 years old. The boy had not been ill, but they found him dead at dawn.

The grief of the people of Upper Egypt is overwhelming, and their funeral prayers are profoundly

7 Bright Saturday commemorates Christ's descent into Hades, out of which He took the righteous in order to bring them to Paradise. It is observed with an overnight prayer vigil that concludes shortly after sunrise with the Divine Liturgy. Resurrection Sunday is celebrated the following day.

sorrowful—especially in cases of sudden death, or when a child passes away. Exhausted, but deeply moved by the heartbreaking news, the priest went. He was like one drugged; he did not comprehend what was happening but moved like a machine that works without understanding. He washed his face, put on his clothes, and went to the church. There, he found the congregation weeping, overcome with sorrow.

This kind priest cried, sharing his people's grief. He stood before the coffin, which was left open according to the custom there, and started praying. First, he prayed the Thanksgiving Prayer. Then, he raised the cross, and, instead of praying the Litany of the Departed, he accidentally prayed the Litany of the Sick; he was still half asleep.[8] As he said, "You have visited them with mercies and compassion, heal them," he saw the boy move in the coffin.

He froze where he stood but continued praying, and the boy's movement increased. The priest shouted, "He is alive!" There was great excitement and joy. They unwrapped the boy. The sorrow disappeared. This happened on Bright Saturday, the day Christ broke the sting of death.

---

8 Litany (from the Greek λιτανεία) means "supplication." Litanies are included throughout the rites and prayers of the Church and are offered for various needs, such as healing for the sick, protection for the travelers, and repose of the departed.

As he was recounting this story, the kind priest said to me, "I could not believe what I saw. My whole body shook." He told me this wondrous story—an incident beyond imagination—as though he had no part in it at all, but was merely a spectator, marveling at the work of God.

He never attributed anything to himself, nor did he consider himself of any significance. He was truly a man of God.

A few years after his release from prison, he suffered a heart attack and departed from the world within seconds. He joined the ranks of the heavenly priests, praising God with the celestial choir that glorifies the Lord unceasingly, without weariness.

CHAPTER TWELVE

The Angel of the Lord Encamps All Around Those Who Fear Him, and Delivers Them

Some of the most marvelous examples of God's care for and protection of His people were experienced by our children during war. Our youth were exposed to certain death, but God saved them miraculously. When they cried to the Lord, He delivered them from trouble and sent His angel at the right time to rescue them.

The First Story

During the war of 1973, I visited His Holiness Pope Shenouda III, and he showed me something extraordinary—a small, pocket-sized book containing the New Testament and the Book of Psalms, pierced in its center by a bullet.[9] The pope said to me, "This book

9 Fr. Louka is referring to the 1973 Arab-Israeli War, also known as the Yom Kippur War, which began on October 6 when Egypt and Syria launched an attack on Israel. The conflict lasted about three weeks.

belonged to one of our soldiers during the war. It was in his left pocket, right over his heart, when this bullet struck. The bullet entered the Gospel and stopped, as you can see. He was saved from death by a miracle."

I marveled. Could the delicate pages of the Gospel really stop a bullet? It was truly miraculous! I said to the pope, "It is as though Jesus put His hand on His son's chest and said to him, 'Leave this to Me. The hand that bore the nails for you will shield you from this harm.'"

Indeed, it has been said of our Lord that "Surely He has borne our griefs And carried our sorrows" (Is 53:4). I pondered how this incident may become a cause for salvation for this brother, who would understand God's love and care and would love the Gospel with a unique love, as it saved him from death.

The Second Story

A similar incident occurred in 1967 involving a young deacon who served at the Church of St. George in Sporting. He was a quiet, spiritual person who loved God and service in God's name. He prayed with an angelic, comforting voice and had many personal experiences with God and His wonderful deeds.

In early June, the young man was unexpectedly enlisted and sent to Sinai. Within a few hours, he found himself among a group of reserves, all called to military service, deep in the desert. The war was imminent, and everything was terrifying.[10] Without warning, Israel launched its attack—sudden and terrible.

Our brother was in a small tent with about 15 other men. They sat in terror, enveloped in a deep, somber silence, as if death itself had taken hold. None of them knew each other.

Each soldier had his own sad life story that, now, would probably end in pain and death. They sat looking at each other, nearly bursting into emotion that no words could express. But then, they looked at our brother and saw his peaceful features. He was evidently different from them all, or at least, so they felt.

One of them shouted to him, "Say something to us!" It was as if he had put his hope in our brother, despite knowing nothing about him.

They were all Muslims, except our Christian brother, who said, "I have the Holy Bible; would you like me to read a passage from it?"

They all answered, like drowning men clinging to anything that might save them, "Read."

He opened the Holy Bible at random; he had no particular passage or aim in mind. He said, "I shall read

---

10 The 1967 war referred to here is commonly called the Six-Day War. It was a brief conflict between Israel and an Arab coalition including Egypt, Syria, and Jordan.

whatever I find before me."

They agreed, and oh, how wonderful! He opened his Bible to the following verse: "Then, the same day at evening, being the first day of the week, when the doors were shut where the disciples were assembled, for fear of the Jews, Jesus came and stood in the midst, and said to them, 'Peace be with you'" (Jn 20:19).

When our brother read these words of grace and comfort, he was filled with Christ's peace. His eyes were bathed in tears of joy—the joy that filled the disciples when they saw the Lord.

When his companions saw him so moved, they asked him for the meaning of what he read. So, he began sharing with them very simply the news of Christ's resurrection and how Christ stood in His disciples' midst and gave them His strength and peace, which took away their fear forever.

The hearts of all these soldiers rejoiced, and they were sure that Immanuel was in their midst, although they did not know Him. They did not understand how they were filled with amazing peace—peace not of this world. Nothing had changed around them, yet they felt something had shifted within them.

Our brother then remembered when St. Paul the Apostle was caught in a severe tempest for 14 days, unable to see the sun. An angel of the Lord stood by him at night and announced to him his safety and the safety of all on board with him. St. Paul proclaimed what the angel of the Lord had said. Then, "he took bread and gave thanks to God in the presence of them all; and when he had broken it he began to eat" (Acts 27:35). He ordered them to eat. They all rejoiced and ate, and God fulfilled His promise. All 276 people on the ship were saved.

When our brother remembered that incident, he said, being confident in God's promises, "Be sure, my friends, God will save us all." They took that promise as God's promise, believed him, and were happy. God, indeed, completed His good work, and they all returned safely—not a hair of their heads was lost (Lk 21:18). This event became a blessing for many.

The Third Story

Another young man told me his story from the war of 1973. He served as an anti-aircraft gun operator, which was very dangerous because the enemy aircrafts focused their attacks on these batteries. Most of this artillery was destroyed in successive air raids, and the soldiers stationed there were often killed by the destructive missiles, resulting in many casualties.

This young man was a servant of Christ. He prayed constantly, asking for the intercessions of the saints. In his wallet, he kept a small icon of the resurrection of our Lord Jesus, another of the Virgin St. Mary, and a third of St. George. During battle, he would stick all three on his gun and have a sense of safety and peace.

The commander of the battalion was a cruel officer. Every time he entered the air-raid shelter and saw those icons, he would mock the young man—sometimes implicitly, other times openly. But our brother bore it all meekly, fixing his gaze on his Master, who, for our sake, "endured the cross, despising the shame" (Heb 12:2).

This young soldier remained strong in his faith and was not afraid or cowardly even for a moment; rather, he clung ever more tightly to God and trusted Him. The war intensified and the anti-aircraft guns were destroyed one after the other. Terror and sorrow gripped everyone, as the number of casualties rose and the defensive strength continued to fall.

From time to time, some of the soldiers would gather in this young man's shelter. Some were fleeing the cannon balls and missiles, looking for any security; others went to this particular shelter because they were sure no harm would come near it as long as the icons of the Lord, glory to Him, the Virgin Mary, and the great martyr St. George were there.

Among those who took refuge in this shelter was the commander. While they were all hiding, the commander turned to our brother and said, "Is this some kind of talisman you've made for your gun?"

The young man, with simple faith and a cheerful spirit, replied, "I thank God. It is He who protects us through His saints. This is greater than any talisman. It is not the strength of man, but the power of God."

The commander was silent for a moment. Then, he responded in a way no one expected: "I believe now. You were right in everything you said and about everything you believe."

From that moment, the commander did not leave the air-raid shelter until the six days of raids were over. Everyone who had gathered in that shelter survived, while all the other shelters belonging to this battalion did not escape destruction. Our brother, therefore, glorified God, who reveals His wonders through His saints.

The Fourth Story

Another soldier I knew loved the Virgin St. Mary and always asked for her intercessions. He grew up in Upper Egypt and was raised by his maternal grandmother, a pious woman whom everybody knew for her wonderful acts. She taught him the way of life with God and dependence on Him. He grew up applying what he learned, setting his heart particularly upon the love of purity and holiness. He often entreated the Virgin Mother to keep him in the life of holiness, without which it is impossible to see the Lord (Heb 12:14).

After he finished high school, he studied engineering at Alexandria University. When he graduated, he was drafted and then spent four years in the military. During the war of 1973, he served with a group of soldiers that included a young officer who deeply despised Christians. After a breach event during which the third Egyptian infantry was besieged, the fanatical officer instigated the whole group to isolate our Christian brother. In response, our brother was patient and asked for the intercessions of the Virgin. He prayed continually, considering the reproach he suffered for Christ to be his greatest reward.

One evening, he woke up at midnight to find no soldiers in his tent or in the surrounding tents. Where had everyone gone? He called out softly but received no answer. He raised his voice and even shouted, but still, there was no response. He thought they must have received an order to retreat, but to where? He did not know which direction to go. He grabbed some necessities (what he could see in the dark), strapped them onto his back, and started running, hoping to find his companions.

He knew that they intentionally did not wake him up, and he feared this location would soon be bombarded, and it would be the end for him. He started running in one direction, not knowing where it would lead; at night in the desert, every direction looks the same. He ended up walking all night and into the day. At last, he found another group of soldiers. Exhausted, he surrendered to the commander of this unit.

The officer asked him, "Where are you from? How did you come here?"

When our brother told him what had happened, the officer said, "Your safety is a miracle. The enemy pursued your unit as they were retreating and annihilated them."

The Christian soldier said to himself what the pure Joseph said to his brothers: "'you meant evil against me; but God meant it for good' [Gen 50:20]."

The New Barsoum

In the 60s, a misunderstanding occurred between some servants at a church in Cairo, causing the disruption of ministries and the loss of many of the church's most enthusiastic servants. These good servants were caused to stumble by those they once held in high regard.

One servant at that church was someone I had known since he graduated university in his 20s. This young man kept his steadfastness, composure, and amazing inner peace throughout the disruptions. The storms did not affect his calm nature or strong faith, nor did they change his love for service and zeal for the salvation of souls. He was like a dove of peace among the quarreling groups, loved and respected by all.

When some of the servants lost their zeal, they gathered from time to time in a house to exchange opinions. They gossiped about church disputes, often criticizing and judging others using abusive language. Their conduct during these meetings caused the Spirit to retreat gradually, until He departed completely. Instead of prayer, their time was spent in idleness. They tried to occupy themselves with games like chess and backgammon. Our loving young man often surprised them with visits, as he was a beloved friend to them all. Whenever he arrived, they would change their behavior, as though the Spirit accompanied Him to their meetings. Their conversations became spiritual and constructive; they meditated and prayed, as if they had regained their early zeal.

This young man was committed, pious, and calm, but never narrow-minded or hypocritical. He loved the Church in an astounding, genuine way and appreciated everything about her: her prayers, her feasts, her rites, her meaning, and even her buildings. He also deeply understood the history of the Church, like one who lived with the saints themselves as their contemporary. The lives of the saints taught him many lessons and were great models for him.

In the mid-60s, he was drafted into the military and entered into a completely new environment. He began to live a life he felt was foreign. He had spent his entire life before this in a religious home, enjoying holiness, spiritual peace, fasting, praise, and prayer. He had always been surrounded by vigilant, devoted church members. Now, he was among very different people. But, by God's grace, he became the light in the darkness and "the salt of the earth" (Mt 5:13). He preserved his spirituality through a life of constant prayer, a heart rising to heaven, and a purity of heart, mind, and tongue. He was a model of life in Christ, never once saying a bad word. God, therefore, was merciful to him and gave him favor in the eyes of all, according to His promises (Ps 5:12).

As time passed and his superiors became well-acquainted with him, they realized he was a man of God. So, whenever they quarreled amongst each other, they went to him to make peace. If they differed in their accounts to the commander, they asked our young soldier to testify, saying to all, "This man does not lie." His presence among them glorified God.

I cannot forget a card I received for Resurrection Sunday, beautifully written with expressive, Christian greetings. To my surprise, the signature was a Muslim name—a fellow soldier in our brother's unit. That conscripted Muslim, a prosecuting attorney I had once met, revealed to me in the card the profound influence our brother had on everyone.

After the 1967 war, our soldiers were stationed on the western bank of the Suez Canal, dwelling in bunkers, while the Israeli soldiers were encamped on the opposite side. That summer was extremely hot, and the sun was scorching. Some of the soldiers would spend time with our brother in his shelter because that brought them peace.

One day, a large snake quietly slithered into our brother's bunker, seeking the shade within. The other soldier in this bunker panicked in fear when he saw it, but our brother calmed him down, saying, "Do not be afraid of this friend who lives with us in peace. He looks for shade, and we shall give him food: an egg or a piece of meat. He will eat and rest, and then, he will go his way."

This happened several times in front of the non-Christian soldiers, who then testified that our brother truly lived with God and was a man of God. Their love and respect for him grew after seeing his living faith.

When these soldiers told me this, I glorified God, who has witnesses at all times and in all places. I said that the Church is alive! St. Barsoum the Naked, who lived with a serpent in the 13th and 14th centuries, is not merely a part of the past.[11] His life, indeed, is living history that can be repeated in our generation and in all generations.

11 St. Barsoum, known as "*El Eryan*" (العريان), meaning "the Naked," is a Coptic saint who embraced asceticism by wearing only a hair sackcloth around his waist, following the example of St. Paul the First Anchorite. He lived for a time in a cave near the Church of St. Philopateer Mercurius in Old Cairo, where a large snake also dwelled. Through his prayers, the snake was tamed, and St. Barsoum affectionately called it "the blessed one."

CHAPTER THIRTEEN

The Purity of Joseph

Is it possible for a young man to live a life of purity in this day and age? Is it really possible to resist temptation and seduction? In an age of increasing freedom, widespread sin, and open immorality, how can one preserve his holiness?

These questions—and many like them—confront people, especially youth, in the midst of their spiritual struggles. They linger, unanswered, in the mind and heart. The call to purity, and the commandments associated with it, may seem more theoretical than practical. Often, a person may even feel it's impossible, beyond the ability of an ordinary Christian, to remain pure. The stories of saints may seem fictional or detached from reality because living a holy life feels out of reach.

So, when a living, contemporary model of purity is found, it speaks louder than a thousand sermons. A life like this has the ability to answer every lingering, confusing question. When we see that living image of purity, we realize that, though the gate is narrow and the way is difficult (Mt 7:14), some have traversed that path and reached their goal; it is difficult but not impossible for others to follow. As Scripture says, "I can do all things through Christ who strengthens me" (Phil 4:13).

Consider the advanced degrees doctors earn in specialized fields or the breakthroughs of engineers, computer scientists, and researchers—achievements that leave others in awe. How did these people reach such heights? Through toil, sleepless nights, and perseverance. The road is difficult but not impossible. Those who came before us were people just like us—or do we think scientists and experts are not made of the same substance we are?

Similarly, in our hope for a better life, the saints are our greatest support because they walked the same path we now walk and, in the end, received their reward. I will mention one young man who left a comforting example, like many other people who have witnessed to Christ at all times and in all places. This young man is one among hundreds I have known who embraced the life of purity, loved holiness, and preserved the chastity of their souls and bodies.

During the 70s, this brother would regularly come to St. George Church in Sporting to confess and attend the youth meetings. He never raised his voice, unlike many other men of his age. He had a radiant face with delicate features like an angel's; God gave him the special blessing of being handsome. He was meek, sensitive, and faithful to Christ. Because of his good-mannered and kind nature, people always wished to be near him, and he maintained good relationships with everyone; his family, teachers, and classmates all loved him.

Moreover, he was outstanding in his academics. After completing his high school education, he studied medicine. Throughout his years at medical school, he was always among the top of his class. He was punctual and disciplined, as well as consistent in his prayer life.

And so, his soul, mind, and heart remained pure. He did not allow any blemish to disturb his purity. His confessions were very specific, and his repentance was sincere. He was quick to confess sins that an ordinary person may not even notice or consider to have any hint of wrongdoing. He was alert and conscientious, and his love for Christ took possession of all his feelings, so that he nurtured a peaceful spirit and grew in holiness.

When he graduated medical school, he became a teaching assistant at the university and a resident physician. He had to stay at the hospital all day and often spend the night, too. From time to time, I would see him at the church's youth meeting. He would listen with all his being to the word of God and partake of the Holy Eucharist the following day.

Sometimes, he would update me about his life after graduation. He shared that he was struggling with a young, beautiful, non-Christian nurse who was giving him excessive attention at work. She was constantly finding reasons to talk to him, sometimes even with flirtatious or inappropriate behavior, though he showed no interest in her. He was prudent, true to God, and continued to love holiness. I encouraged him to pray often, especially using the Jesus Prayer—the Constant Prayer—because, through the name of our Savior, our Lord Jesus Christ, demons are cast out and flames are extinguished.[12] He was obedient and faithful in practicing this prayer, and so, he experienced inner joy and peace. When he came to me again, he was calm and reassured.

But as time passed, the nurse's advances toward him intensified; she seemed to chase him around everywhere. He was distressed, but, the more he ignored her, the more persistent she became, driven by the devil.

One day, he came to me burdened, unsure of what to do. I told him, "We have no weapons but prayer and fasting. These strengthen us and uphold us by grace, for the Lord said, 'this kind does not go out except by prayer and fasting' [Mt 17:21]—and, as the Lord said, heaven and earth will pass away, but His words will by no means

12 The Jesus Prayer, also known as the "Arrow Prayer" or the "Constant Prayer," is a short, simple prayer that many Orthodox Christians repeat throughout the day. It is usually prayed as a variation of: "Lord Jesus Christ, Son of God, have mercy on me, a sinner." Like an arrow shot quickly toward a target, this prayer is a brief but powerful way to reach out to God at any moment.

pass away [Mt 24:35]. Do you fast on Wednesdays and Fridays?"[13]

"Yes," he answered.

"Then, let's add a third day."

So, he began fasting on Wednesday, Thursday, and Friday every week, abstaining from food for a few hours and committing himself to fervent prayer.

A few weeks passed, and then, one night, he and the nurse were scheduled to work the same overnight shift. After midnight, once the ward was quiet, he retreated to his room, prayed a few of the twelfth hour psalms of the *Agpeya*, and lay down to rest, hoping for a bit of sleep before any patient emergencies arose. He drifted into a peaceful sleep, protected by an angel of peace.

Suddenly, he was jolted awake by a woman's scream. Alarmed, he got up and ran toward the sound, following it to one of the rooms. He rushed inside and found the nurse naked and alone. Satan had set a trap to ensnare him, filling the woman's heart and inflaming her mind with evil. For months, she had tried every means of seduction, but our young physician had given her no

13 The Coptic Church fasts on Wednesdays and Fridays throughout the year, except during the Holy Fifty Days following the Feast of the Resurrection, and when the Feasts of the Nativity or Theophany fall on a Wednesday or Friday. Wednesday commemorates Judas's betrayal and conspiracy against Christ, and Friday commemorates Christ's death on the cross for the salvation of humanity.

attention. When the devil is defeated, he goes mad—and this was his last desperate trick.

Nevertheless, the power of fasting and prayer, the blessing of vigilance, and the love of Christ rescued him. Sin is not attractive—it is repulsive; "How then can I do this great wickedness, and sin against God?" (Gen 39:9).

He made the sign of the life-giving cross, and God granted him amazing strength. She locked the door and stood in front of it to block his escape. He gently pushed her aside, not using much force at all. He did not understand how, but, somehow, she collapsed to the ground. There was a hidden, unusual power acting. He opened the door and ran out, glorifying the Almighty God and the cross, which is "foolishness to those who are perishing, but to us who are being saved it is the power of God" (1 Cor 1:18).

He left the hospital and came to my house before dawn. He apologized for coming so early; he couldn't wait until the morning. I was surprised to see him, but how I rejoiced with him when he told me what happened! I glorified our wonderful God, the Almighty. We prayed the first hour psalms of the *Agpeya* together with joy. The sweet taste of triumph is wonderful beyond words! Just as falling into sin is bitter, overcoming it is deeply joyful and satisfying, when a person feels the arms of Christ embracing him. I prayed for him with all my heart, and I said, "Truly, 'The angel of the Lord encamps all around those who fear Him, And delivers them' [Ps 34:7]."

"Oh, taste and see that the Lord is good; Blessed is the man who trusts in Him!" (Ps 34:8).

ⲠⲒⲠⲀⲦⲢⲒⲀⲢⲬⲎⲔ ⲒⲰⲤⲎⲪ

✠

CHAPTER FOURTEEN

May the Lord Answer You in the Day of Trouble

This young, kind-hearted Christian man was raised in a devout family in El-Minya Governorate. He was a model of obedience and good character. His excellent grades in high school earned him admission to the Qasr Al-Ainy Faculty of Medicine at Cairo University in the early 1950s. Despite his family's limited financial means, they insisted he travel to this school to complete his studies.

His older sister, who was unmarried, accompanied him. They rented a small room in Giza together. He was diligent in his studies, and the family, despite its modest resources, sent them 3 pounds every month to cover the university fees, as well as their rent and living expenses. This amount was a significant burden on the family, but they thanked God and focused on their son's future. Such sacrifice for the sake of a child's education was the norm for most Coptic families.

He became deeply connected to the church in Giza,

finding in it a home, as the psalmist writes: "Even the sparrow has found a home, And the swallow a nest for herself, Where she may lay her young—Even Your altars, O Lord of hosts, My King and my God. Blessed are those who dwell in Your house" (Ps 84:3–4). He regularly attended liturgies, youth meetings, and servants meetings. The late Hegumen Fr. Salib Suryal was a compassionate and loving spiritual father to whom he clung closely, consulting him on every matter, big or small, and not taking a single step without seeking his fatherly advice.

Months passed, and the young man was adapting to his new life at his university, church, and apartment. He prayed often and was very thankful for the money he received every month from his parents.

One month in winter, he waited for the money order to arrive in the mail, but it never came. It would usually arrive at the beginning of the month, but a week passed with nothing. His and his sister's provisions dwindled, and they were close to running out. They had no other source of income and no relatives in Cairo. He was also far too shy to ask anyone for help; who would even give him anything anyway?

He and his sister began to ration the little food they had left, while continuing to pray and ask for God's help. Eventually, they ran out of everything—they did not even have a single loaf of bread. His sister grew anxious. As he was about to head out for university one morning, she said to him, "Don't come back without finding a way to help us, or we will starve."

On the young man's walk to the university, tears streamed down his face as he lifted his eyes to heaven, praying, "You feed the young ravens when they call upon You [Ps 147:9]. 'You open Your hand And satisfy the desire of every living thing' [Ps 145:16]." Then, he prayed Psalm 20, which begins with, "May the Lord answer you in the day of trouble." He found great comfort in these words.

After he prayed, he did not know what to do. With a broken heart, he asked for God's guidance. Should he go to university and ask a colleague for help or a loan? Should he send a telegram to his parents? But where would he get the money for that? Finally, it occurred to him to go to Fr. Salib and ask for his help. He felt very embarrassed, but what was the alternative?

While lost in these thoughts, he reached Giza Square. He stood in the middle of the square, as if at a crossroads, unsure of where to turn. Lifting his tearful eyes to heaven again, he cried, "'How long, O Lord?' [Ps 13:1]."

As he lowered his gaze, a piece of paper caught his attention, carried by the wind. The paper flew and hit his leg, sticking to his pants. He bent down to remove it, and, to his utter amazement, he discovered it was not an ordinary piece of paper; it was a banknote for 1 pound. He couldn't believe his eyes and stood frozen.

He thought, *Could this pound have flown out of someone's hand?* He held the pound and raised it high, waiting for whoever lost it to come claim it. He stood for a minute, his hand raised, looking around, but no one approached him or asked him about it. He was overwhelmed with emotion and nearly shouted aloud about how the Lord had answered immediately and miraculously! Afraid of drawing attention and being mistaken for someone deranged, he quickly left the spot.

In awe, he thanked God with all his heart. His heart overflowed with thanksgiving, and tears poured down his face uncontrollably. He couldn't form words, for his heart was brimming with gratitude beyond expression.

He continued on his way. *To where?* he thought. *To the church. I must give the tithe.*

He stopped by a grocer to buy a few essentials and then headed to the church to put 10 piasters in the offering box. As he entered, he encountered Fr. Salib, who saw his state, embraced him lovingly, and asked, "What's wrong, my son?"

The young man shared his story in detail, concluding by saying, "And now, I'm here to give the tithe."

Fr. Salib said, "What tithe, my son? Keep what little you have until the Lord provides relief."

But the young man insisted, saying, "Father, please, let me ease my conscience."

Fr. Salib marveled at his extraordinary faith and allowed him to do as he wished. Then, the young man returned home, glorifying God, and recounted the Lord's miraculous work to his sister. Their little provisions were blessed wonderfully, and, since that day, this young man lacked nothing because the Lord blessed him.

He graduated from medical school, and God's hand was with him throughout his life. As a doctor, he remained as he always had been—generous and compassionate to the poor. The Lord blessed him with countless blessings and worked many wonders throughout his life's journey.

✠

CHAPTER FIFTEEN

The Simple Mikhail

Among those who came for confession, I would see Mikhail from time to time, sitting silently as he waited his turn. He was truly a man of prayer. He would intentionally wait until he was the last of the confessors, which meant sitting in the church for two or three hours before his confession. He worked as a construction laborer, and his appearance was simple—so simple that one would perhaps feel inclined to give him alms.

Through listening to his confessions, I saw in him a soul that was simple yet enlightened. He spent his days carrying baskets filled with sand or gravel and lifting troughs of mixed concrete from morning till evening. It is well-known that the environment of physical laborers is a difficult one; many laborers have morals and ways of speaking that make interactions extremely challenging, often leading to loud, violent quarrels that could involve construction tools. It is an environment where it seems almost impossible to maintain peace or nurture any sort of spiritual life.

Yet, Mikhail, by the grace of God, was able to work

in this environment while growing in grace and spiritual stature. He practiced unceasing prayer in the midst of his surroundings. Despite his simple outward appearance, inwardly, he had a deeply profound love for Christ and relationship with God. He had memorized the *Agpeya* by heart, having learned the prayers as a child in his village's church school in Upper Egypt. He was joyful and content, practicing his prayers in secret, retreating with God, and paying no attention to what people said about him. He was, despite everything around him, peaceful toward all, always serving others with extraordinary humility. His life was completely shaped by prayer.

One day, he came to me, burdened with persistent thoughts of leaving the world. He felt that being among people had become too heavy to bear. His daily work hours seemed like wasted time with no benefit. Why not devote all his time to undistracted prayer? He desired nothing, sought nothing, and hoped for nothing from the world—so why should he remain in it?

These thoughts had been chasing him for some time, but now they had become relentless. Each time he came to me with these thoughts, I explained to him that leaving the world required a complete and unwavering intent, an undivided heart, and a clear goal. A person seeking to follow this path must test himself and count the cost, as advised by the Desert Fathers. He would always listen to me quietly, obeying with simple trust, without argument or debate.

But this time, he pleaded with tears. The world had become an unbearable burden for him. His intention was entirely free from any desire for recognition, status, or outward appearance. He did not seek to wear monastic robes, to receive a new name, or anything of the sort.[14] He simply wanted to live as a servant in the monastery—nothing more.

Seeing the sincerity of his heart, I wrote a letter to Fr. Mina Ava Mina explaining Mikhail's situation and his deep desire to live in the monastery. Fr. Mina accepted him and, as Mikhail wished, gave him a small room at the monastery's gate.

How immense was Mikhail's joy! He had finally received what his heart had been longing for. How he delighted in the morning prayers and hymns, and how he was comforted by the daily liturgies! Truly, this was his paradise on earth.

One night, after completing the evening prayers, he retired to his modest room. He lit a candle and

---

14 In the Coptic tradition, when one is consecrated as a monastic, he or she receives a new name and a monastic robe consisting of a black cassock, a black head covering, and a leather belt. These changes indicate that the "old things have passed away" (2 Cor 5:17) and this person has "put on the new man which was created according to God, in true righteousness and holiness" (Eph 4:24). For more on Coptic monasticism, refer to *On the Monastic Life* by Pope Shenouda III.

continued praying the midnight hour psalms of the *Agpeya* until late into the night. As tiredness overcame him, he unknowingly fell asleep while kneeling on his small cotton mattress, the lit candle still in his hand. The candle fell, setting the mattress on fire.

One can imagine how quickly cotton ignites, burning in mere seconds. As this was happening, he remained fast asleep, completely unaware of the danger. The smell of smoke filled the air, reaching some brothers in the distance. They hurried to the scene.

To their astonishment, Brother Mikhail's room was filled with smoke. They called out to him, raising their voices until he finally awoke. When they got a lantern and entered, what they saw was extraordinary—the fire had burned the entire mattress except for the small section on which he was lying. That part remained untouched, as if the fire had been restricted by an invisible boundary. His clothes had not burned; not even the scent of fire clung to them. Not a single hair on his head was singed.

Everyone was bewildered by this miraculous sight. It was as if he were one of the three youths in the fiery furnace (Dan 3:8–25)—how had he remained unharmed? They gave thanks to God. Mikhail, however, reproached himself, feeling guilty that his negligence and sleepiness had caused such a situation. Some of the brothers feared that his carelessness might bring trouble, so they sent him back to Alexandria.

He came to me sorrowful, but I comforted him and assigned him to serve at the Church of Archangel Michael. He worked there as a devoted servant, later moving to serve at St. Mark Church. Years passed, and, eventually, the Lord granted him rest from the toils of this fleeting world. He departed to join the ranks of the righteous—those whom the world is not worthy to keep.

✠

CHAPTER SIXTEEN

The Cross Is the Power of God

Among the most painful sights that move a man to pity are those tormented by unclean spirits. Truly, how astounding are the accounts of those who lived among the tombs, like the man who cried out and cut himself with stones (Mk 5:1–20), or the story of the boy whom the demon would throw into seizures, causing him to foam at the mouth and convulse (Mk 9:14–29)? These are images of humanity suffering under the weight of the one who, from the beginning, has been a murderer of souls (Jn 8:44).

In ancient times, when humanity was primitive in thought and understanding, focused more on the body than the mind, the devil would often control people by inhabiting their bodies, tormenting them and ultimately leading them to ruin. But as human intellect developed and became inventive, the devil's warfare shifted to target the mind. If the devil succeeds in captivating one's mind, he gains control over the entire being. For this reason, it is rarer today to find people possessed by unclean spirits in their bodies. In modern societies, the devil dominates thoughts, leading people into all kinds of evil without the need for direct control over their bodies.

The First Story

In the late 1960s, I was with a group of servants in the church during a servants meeting. At around 6 in the evening, four men entered the church. At first glance, it was clear they were not locals and were not Christians. They asked for assistance, and one of the servants guided them further into the church. They were accompanying an elderly man, about 70 years old, who appeared extremely frail and on the verge of fainting.

I hurried to meet them, seated the elderly man, and asked them what they needed and how I could be of help. They explained that they were not Christians but had heard of the great martyr St. George. They said that the elderly man was possessed by an unclean spirit that had been tormenting him for years. Recently, the torment had intensified to a degree that was killing him, as the spirit prevented him from eating or drinking.

I had never encountered anything like this before in my life; this was my first time seeing someone possessed by an unclean spirit. I asked, "How is this possible?"

They said, "He speaks in strange voices and languages we don't understand."

I asked, "Why doesn't he eat? The man is extremely

frail."

They said, "For three days, he hasn't eaten anything. Whenever we bring food to him, the demon clenches his teeth and swells his stomach, making it impossible for him to open his mouth or for us to feed him. Look at the state he's in—utter misery and suffering."

I looked at the man; his condition was truly pitiful. I thought to myself, *Lord, could humanity really fall prey to this cruel enemy to this extent? Can Your creation be so mocked and humiliated by the one who has been a murderer from the beginning?* As I listened to their story, I felt fearful and cautious, unsure of what to do. I was young at the time and lacked experience in such matters. I turned to one of the servants standing nearby and said, "Go quickly and get some sandwiches from the shop next to the church." The servant returned within minutes, carrying the food.

I offered the poor old man a sandwich, and what I saw was astonishing; the man's teeth immediately locked loudly in fear, his stomach swelled like a balloon, and his eyes shut. It was an absolutely horrifying sight. The servants stood around me in shock and fear. I was holding a small cross in my hand, and, instinctively, I placed the cross on the man's swollen stomach. To my astonishment, his stomach immediately returned to its normal state, and he opened his eyes and mouth. I offered him the food again. The poor man said, "Please, leave that thing you've placed on my stomach—don't take it away, I beg you." He did not recognize it as the cross. He devoured the food ravenously, as if he were starving to death.

After he finished eating, I showed him the cross and explained our faith in it, saying, "'For the message of the cross is foolishness to those who are perishing, but to us who are being saved it is the power of God' [1 Cor 1:18]." I gave him a small cross and said, "Keep this with you. Wear it on your chest, and the devil will not be able to harm you."

One of the servants then began repeating the saving name of our Lord Jesus Christ, saying, "Lord Jesus, Lord Jesus, Lord Jesus."

Suddenly, the man began to speak in a hoarse voice, unlike his natural one, saying, "Oh, Jesus."

I said to him, "Be silent! Do you know Jesus?"

He replied, "How could I not know Him? I know Jesus Christ very well."

Indeed, it is written, "And demons also came out of many, crying out and saying, 'You are the Christ, the Son of God!' And He, rebuking them, did not allow them to speak, for they knew that He was the Christ" (Lk 4:41). Demons know that He is the Holy One, who triumphed over them on the cross, making a public spectacle of them.

The Second Story

Another time, a taxicab suddenly stopped in front of the church gate as we were greeting the congregation at the entrance after the Divine Liturgy. Three men flung the car doors open and hurriedly got out, as though fleeing from danger. They were visibly exhausted and covered in bloody wounds. Their appearance alarmed the people gathered outside the church, who rushed to the taxi, trying to understand what had happened.

I, too, approached and found in the taxi a terrified and agitated woman. The three men said that she was possessed by a demon. She had attacked the men with her nails and teeth, leaving them severely wounded, and, despite their combined strength, they could not restrain her. The taxi driver was even more frightened than these men because he only realized her condition after she had already gotten into the car.

I got closer to the door of the cab, but the *qarabni* of the church, a servant named Amm Bishay, quickly got behind me and tried to prevent me from getting any nearer, afraid I might get hurt.[15] I said to him, "Oh, Amm Bishay, the devil is afraid of the cross." Holding the holy cross in my hand, I extended my arm towards that poor

15 The Arabic term *qarabni* (قربني), stemming from *qurban*, "offering," is a traditional Coptic Orthodox title referring to the servant entrusted with preparing the Eucharistic bread for the Divine Liturgy.

woman who was behaving like a mad dog. The moment her eyes fell upon the cross, she lowered her gaze, and an astonishing calm overtook her. This happened in the blink of an eye.

I helped her out of the cab and took her inside the church. She knelt down on the ground and began dragging herself on her knees. Those who had accompanied her were astonished. I told them that the cross terrifies the demons. I gave them an example from *The Paradise of the Holy Fathers*: a dog used to snatch pieces of meat from a butcher, so the butcher gave the dog a painful beating with a stick, and the dog remembered that beating, so that every time he saw the butcher extending his hand toward the stick, he ran in terror.[16]

They asked, "What does that mean?"

I answered, "The devil did not and will never forget the day when Christ crushed him with the cross. That day, Christ humiliated Satan and destroyed his power. Christ trampled down death by death. He rose, breaking the sting of death. Since that day, Satan has been afraid of the cross and even the name and sign of the cross."

---

16 *The Paradise of the Holy Fathers*, known in Arabic as *Bustan al-Ruhban* (بستان الرهبان), is a compilation of the lives, sayings, and spiritual teachings of early Desert Fathers—monks, anchorites, and ascetics like St. Anthony the Great and St. Moses the Strong—who lived in the deserts of Egypt between 250 and 400 A.D.

The Third Story

A hermit once told me about a time a demon-possessed man was brought to the monastery, tormented severely by an evil spirit. Those who brought him waited with him until Vespers ended and then took him to one of the fathers. They said that he had not had anything to drink for two days. The father brought a pitcher of water, and, without the man seeing, traced the sign of the life-giving cross over it before handing it to him. The moment the man received the pitcher, he hurled it away with great force, shattering it to pieces, and refused to drink. The father then asked for another pitcher. Once again, he made the sign of the cross over it before giving it to the man, and, just as before, the man angrily threw it aside and broke it. Finally, the father requested a third pitcher but did not bless it this time. When he handed it to the man, the man drank from it without hesitation.

At that moment, the father was certain—it was the demon who feared the sign of the cross. With divine authority, the father questioned the spirit, "Do you have power over him? How dare you enter and dwell in a Christian?"

The unclean spirit answered, "Because he does not partake of the Eucharist."

The father asked, "For how long?"

The spirit answered, "For more than 40 days."

"So you know the laws of the church?"[17]

"Yes."

"What about those who are not Christians?"

"I enter them at birth."

To this extent, the devil knows our weaknesses and understands the power of the Divine Mysteries. He trembles at the sign of the cross, the sign of salvation, which is the pride of Christians.

The Fourth Story

Fr. Bishoy Kamel told me about an incident that occurred early in his ministry at St. George Church in Sporting. He was not yet well-known among the congregation, and the church at the time was modest, constructed of red bricks with a simple roof. At the entrance was an icon of the great martyr St. George with an oil lamp lit in front of it. One day, a man and woman of visibly wealthy appearance entered the church hesitantly, with great politeness and humility. They asked, "Is there a priest here named Fr. Bishoy?" Fr. Bishoy welcomed them warmly and inquired about the reason for their visit. They explained that they were wealthy residents of the area, living close to the

17 According to Coptic tradition, not partaking of the Eucharist for an extended period of time, traditionally 40 days or more, leaves Christians more prone to demonic influences both mentally and physically.

church, but they were not Christians. They had a son who had been possessed by an unclean spirit for some time, and, despite all their efforts, his condition kept worsening. They had sought help from fortune tellers and spiritual healers, but nothing had worked. Their sorrow was immense, and they were utterly desperate. They had heard the demon inside their son say, "I will not leave unless Fr. Bishoy brings cotton soaked in the oil from St. George's lamp."

They asked, "What is that lamp? And who is St. George?"

So, Fr. Bishoy explained to them the life and miracles of the great martyr. They also noticed that St. George held a spear in his icon and asked about it.

Fr. Bishoy answered, "It symbolizes the cross, the power of God through which we overcome Satan."

They implored Fr. Bishoy to go with them to their son. So, he took a piece of cotton, dipped it in the oil of St. George's lamp, and went with them. He made the sign of the cross on the young man's forehead with the piece of cotton. The young man was immediately cured, and all who were present glorified God for His great deeds through His saints.

✠

CHAPTER SEVENTEEN

Poor, but Rich in Faith

"Has God not chosen the poor of this world to be rich in faith and heirs of the kingdom?" (Jas 2:5). My faith in these words of the apostle James deepened when the grace of God allowed me to see and interact with many poor people. I loved their pure, unpretentious faith, declared openly and without hypocrisy. I saw how their poverty did not harm their spirits, which resembled that of their Savior, who was born in a manger and had no place to lay His head (Mt 8:20).

The First Story

A poor widow in her mid-60s came to church every Monday to attend the Divine Liturgy. Fr. Bishoy Kamel had a special concern for the poor, so he dedicated Mondays to serving them. After the liturgy, he would divide them into groups and assign certain women in the congregation to serve them—teaching them hymns, studying the Bible with them, and singing with them.

This poor widow came regularly and partook of the

Holy Communion. Her life in Christ was calm and gentle, like a soft breeze. Every Monday, she received a small blessing from the church: 25 piasters, along with any food, fruit, oil, or other provisions God had provided to be distributed among the poor.

One day, Fr. Bishoy came to me very emotional and said, "Do you know Om [he stated her eldest son's name], the poor widow?"

I answered, "Yes, of course I know her."

He said, "I was visiting some of the poor in the Hadra district, who guided me to a very poor shack. Inside, I found an elderly man who was disabled—his condition was heartbreaking. I asked the others to step outside, gave him some money, and offered to arrange for someone to bring him what he needed every week. Will you believe what he told me? The man said, 'No, Father, I thank God. Every week, Om so-and-so [the poor widow] brings me 15 piasters and plenty of food.'"

Fr. Bishoy said that he could hardly believe what he had heard. How did that poor widow give the man more than half of what she received from the church? She had no income and was given charity, but she could still do charitable deeds. There is thus no limit to acts of kindness; "Has God not chosen the poor of this world to be rich in faith" (Jas 2:5)? Truly, this widow is richer than the wealthy.

The Second Story

One morning, Fr. Bishoy met me with his radiant smile and said, "Yesterday, there was a scene in our house you would have loved to witness. You know the lady Shams?"

I replied, "Of course, I know her—she is a poor woman who sells vegetables in the market."

"Her old building collapsed completely, leaving her and her children homeless. The authorities took them to a mosque where they spent the night. The imam of the mosque approached her and said, 'You are a Christian. Are you comfortable sleeping here?' She replied, 'I am the daughter of Fr. Bishoy, and he taught us to love everyone and that we are all brothers and sisters.' The imam thanked her, saying, 'Indeed, this is how we should all live—in love and peace.'"

Fr. Bishoy continued, "The following night—last night—she came to our house from the market and told us what happened. 'Everything I owned is now buried beneath rubble,' she said, 'but all these things are temporary. I thank God for His gifts.' My wife, Angel, told Shams she must stay with us and gave her food. Shams ate, thanking God. When it came time to sleep, Angel asked Shams to sleep on the bed, but Shams adamantly refused. She said, 'My clothes are dirty. My feet are filthy from walking barefoot in the muddy market. I can't dirty your sheets.' Angel insisted, and they began to quarrel.

Shams was adamant, and Angel tried to pull her to the bed."

I said, "How did that end?"

"They both ended up sleeping on the floor the whole night," he said, laughing. "The next morning, Angel tried to give Shams a few necessities, but the woman was amazingly meek. She has nothing—no home or possessions. She lost every necessity, but she did not lose her satisfaction in Christ. She was full—and her fullness came from God."

I then thought about the rich, who are often ungrateful and complain, and greed, which ruins so many lives. And I remembered the verse, "There is one who makes himself rich, yet has nothing; And one who makes himself poor, yet has great riches" (Prov 13:7).

The Third Story

I knew a young man who was born with disabilities; he spoke very little and stuttered, so one could hardly understand what he was saying. He looked like an old man, and his clothes were very worn. He drooled all over himself, so some saw him as repulsive. His abilities were few, but the poor young man had a heart full of zeal to serve the needy. He deeply loved Christ and the poor, the brothers of the Lord.

Many who saw his appearance would offer him

money, assuming he was in need. But later, we came to know that he was the son of a well-off man—a wholesale fruit merchant—and that he lacked nothing. More than that, we learned that this brother was noble-hearted and generous in giving. He would receive large sums from his father, a man of great kindness, and use them to serve the poor. His father rejoiced that the Lord had compensated his son's physical limitations with an abundance of spirit and devotion to Christ's service. The young man knew many poor families by name. If he happened to find some of them at church seeking help, he would quietly approach the priest and whisper in his ear things like, "This woman is in great need; give her a blessing. That one over there is doing well—she can manage."

Once, I was at the Monastery of St. Mina, where I was surprised to see a large bus arrive, packed with poor people. Women and children poured out of it, joyful and full of praise. This brother had arranged the entire trip for them. He had gathered the funds to rent the bus, asked one of the church members to handle the rental since he himself did not know how, and organized the women and their children at the church before taking them on the pilgrimage to the monastery. Not a single one of them had paid a penny. He organized these trips for the poor families several times, bringing a new group each time, so that more could share in the blessing. He took upon himself all the expenses and repeated, "They are all poor. Jesus loves them. Jesus loves the children of the poor."

He acted with the simplicity of a child, wisdom from above, and a heart full of love. He carried baskets of food and fruit on his back and walked long distances, knocking at poor families' doors to offer them what he had. He walked the streets all day, serving Christ with his limited ability.

The appearance and conduct of this young man humbled the greatest servants and priests. His behavior teaches a lesson in humility: "'Not by might nor by power, but by My Spirit,' Says the Lord of hosts" (Zech 4:6).

Cheerfulness in Giving

Another story I remember is about a destitute man who used to pray at the Church of the Virgin Mary and St. Cyril the Great in Cleopatra District, Alexandria. He was humble in his spirit, appearance, and all aspects of his life. His clothes were tattered and worn. He had been a laborer who worked with his hands to earn his daily bread, but, after injuring one of his eyes and developing a heart condition, he could no longer do manual labor. As a result, he had no source of income.

The moment he would enter the church for prayer, he would go straight to the sanctuary, pouring out his tears and supplications before God. He prayed the Holy

Liturgy with all his heart and mind. In his piety and love for Christ, he had memorized all the responses and would pray them in a soft voice. No matter how great his need, he would never accept anything from anyone inside the church. For him, the church was the house of prayer. I could hardly give him any money because, though he was in dire need, his faith in Christ gave him constant satisfaction.

One day, after the liturgy, I saw him standing in confusion. By then, the church was nearly empty—most of the congregation had left. He remained behind, looking around anxiously.

I asked him, "What's wrong?"

He replied, "I can't find my shoes."

I looked around and found only a single pair. It looked new and unworn. I said, "Perhaps these are yours?"

He shook his head. "No."

"Everyone has left, and this is the only pair remaining. Take it and go."

But he refused. "I can't. My shoes were old and worn out. This new pair does not belong to me."

I insisted, but he steadfastly declined. So I said, "Wait a little longer—perhaps, someone will realize they took yours by mistake and come back to the church."

He waited for over half an hour, but no one came.

Then, at last, he said, "Forgive me, Father, I have to go."

When I looked down, I saw that he was barefoot.

I asked, "Why didn't you take the shoes?"

He replied, "I can't."

At that moment, I took the shoes, pressed them into his hands, and made him wear them against his will.

A few days later, one of the deacons told me that he saw a certain man wearing the poor man's old, tattered shoes after Communion. This man hurried out of the church soon afterward.

I told the deacon, "Perhaps he wore them by mistake."

I then went to visit the kind man to talk to him privately. I asked him, "What happened so that you took the poor man's shoes?"

He asked, "Who told you this?"

I replied, "I just knew."

The good man said, "I do not understand that man. He is obviously very poor, but I tried several times to give him money, and he refused. After church, we offered him food, but he just smiled and said, 'Thank you, my beloved. Jesus Christ cares even for the ravens—He feeds them' [Lk 12:24]. I was silent and amazed, but I wanted with all my heart to give him any help. Then, last Sunday, I had this rare opportunity. After I received Communion, I saw the poor man's old torn shoes, so I put them on and left the church quickly, leaving behind my shoes, which I had only used a few times. I left the church so happy to have given this brother of Christ something not worth mentioning."

That day, I glorified Christ and His Spirit acting in us in this manner: moving the giver to give and giving the needy a feeling of satisfaction. The Church is, indeed, rich in the faith of her children.

CHAPTER EIGHTEEN

Watering the Spirit

One engineer and his wife were among the many shining examples of devout Christian families. Their home felt like a small church in every sense of the word. Spiritual peace was the general atmosphere in which this blessed family lived. All the servants of the Lord, including bishops, priests, and deacons, found rest and comfort in that home, especially Bishop Youannis of Al-Gharbia and Fr. Bishoy Kamel. The word of God was the center of every visit, and hymns and praises filled every corner of the house. It was a place of true, inexpressible joy.

From time to time, the couple would visit Fr. Sadek, who lived on the same street as them, and their souls found rest together in the abundance of the word of God. Grace showered gifts over them. Fr. Sadek considered them his most beloved children because, whenever they heard the word, they stored it in their pure hearts, bearing the fruit of the Spirit.

The couple was certain that God's grace had provided them with extraordinary heavenly blessings.

They had two children—a son and a daughter—who grew up in this spiritual environment and, therefore, were remarkably calm and meek. Their purity remained with them permanently, even after they grew up and graduated from university.

Because of her children and household responsibilities, the woman had a live-in maid—a girl of about 12 years old from a poor, rural, non-Christian family. Though she was not a Christian, the couple treated her with extraordinary kindness and love, to the point that they considered her their eldest daughter. In every way, she was treated as a member of the family, even dressing like the family. When they sat down to eat, the woman would prepare the maid's plate before her own.

Whether they were going out or staying home, they were always together. As the girl matured into a young woman, she absorbed the spirit of the family and chose of her own will to live the same holy life. She fasted all the Church fasts, including Wednesdays and Fridays, and even joined the woman in her personal fasts. The woman tried in vain to dissuade her, saying, "These fasts and prayers are not of your faith, nor the faith of your parents." But the girl remained steadfast. She had fallen in love with the Lord—whom she had heard about so often, but more importantly, whom she had witnessed with her own eyes in the life of her mistress. There was simply no comparison between what she had seen in the outside world and what she experienced under the roof of this family. She felt as though she were living in heaven, or a dream, in a place unlike any other in the world. Her life was overflowing with holiness and joy.

One particular scene remains engraved in my mind, despite more than a quarter of a century having passed. One day, a group of us, including Fr. Bishoy, went with Bishop Youannis to visit the family. The woman got up and went to the kitchen to prepare something for her guests. Immediately, her maid rushed to stop her, insisting that she would do it instead. But the woman said to her, "No, you go sit and listen to the word of God. I'll do this." The girl insisted, "No—you sit! This is *my* job." The woman refused. When Bishop Youannis overheard their conversation, he quickly went to the kitchen to find them arguing. Amazed, he said, "Neither of you will do anything—come, let's all pray and read the Bible, and, when we're done, you can go and prepare what you like." To such an extent, humility and love were practiced in this household.

What is remarkable is that, when the maid's parents passed away and her relatives came to take her to marry one of their sons, she firmly refused, saying, "I have chosen my path."

They said to her, "Your parents died."

She looked at the couple and said, "These are my parents. I live the happiest life under their protection."

So, her relatives left her alone. In time, God blessed this servant with His adoption, completing her joy in Christ. She was special among Christians because, when she came to partake of the Holy Communion, she came craving the Spring of Life.

Indeed, the Spirit is like a drink of water; we "have all been made to drink into one Spirit," (1 Cor 12:13) running like water. This is the mystery of life in the Spirit—a life that flows with sincerity, where faith pervades without hindrance. It is piety like a seed sown in the earth, bearing fruit—30, 60, and a hundredfold. Did not the Spirit flow from Cornelius to all those around him, even to the soldiers under his command (Acts 10)?

Grace abounded in this young maid's life. In time, she was joined in Holy Matrimony to a devout young man who lived the Christian life. She, too, established her own small church, modeled after the example she had witnessed and experienced in the loving embrace of her beloved spiritual family.

✠

CHAPTER NINETEEN

A Heavenly Reception

I first met Mr. Ghobrial in 1967. He served in the army, holding the high rank of Colonel. He was simple in nature, had a kind heart, and knew nothing of deceit, cunning, or guile. He acted with spontaneity, spoke in a loud voice, and was frank with everyone. After being placed in the reserves, his life became almost entirely devoted to God—studying the Gospel, reading spiritual books, regularly partaking in the sacraments, attending all evening prayers without fail, and performing acts of charity both within his family and the church community. He was beloved by Fr. Bishoy Kamel and all the priests of the church.

In late 1971, Pope Shenouda III, after being enthroned as the Patriarch of the See of St. Mark, made his first visit to Alexandria and to the Church of St. George in Sporting. It was a memorable day; the church, including its entrances, ground floor, and even surrounding streets, was packed with multitudes of people, all eager to welcome the pope on his first papal visit and receive his apostolic blessing. At that time, Fr. Tadros Malaty served in Los Angeles, and we were hoping for his return to the Church of St. George. Fr. Bishoy planned to ask the pope for Fr. Tadros's reassignment on behalf of the congregation.

Many wished to offer words of welcome and love to the pope, including Colonel Ghobrial. His son lived in Los Angeles, and, for this reason, Fr. Bishoy feared that Ghobrial might speak in favor of keeping Fr. Tadros in the U.S., noting his fruitful ministry there. Ghobrial was well-informed on all the U. S. news through his son.

Fr. Bishoy said to me, "I am afraid Mr. Ghobrial will speak."

I was the one to introduce the speakers. I whispered in the pope's ear, "Many people would like to speak. Shall we limit it to just a few due to time constraints?"

The pope replied, "Do as you see fit."

I then approached Ghobrial and said, "We don't have much time, so we're limiting speakers to three, followed by Fr. Bishoy, then the pope's address."

He asked, "And I will speak?"

I replied, "No, you will not be speaking."

Raising his voice, he insisted, "I will ask the pope for permission—I must speak."

I responded firmly, "I told you, you will not speak."

He grew upset, rose from his seat, and left the church

loudly, greatly affected by the situation.

This drew the attention of the pope, who asked, "What is it?"

I explained, "He wanted to speak, but I told him that, due to time constraints, only three speakers are allowed, so he became upset and left."

The pope gently replied, "It is alright. You can talk to him later."

The scheduled speakers said their remarks, followed by Fr. Bishoy, who mentioned the situation with Fr. Tadros in the middle of his speech. Then, the pope spoke, addressing the congregation with words of spiritual grace that filled them with joy. He also alluded to Fr. Tadros's return. The Vespers concluded peacefully, with no further disruptions.

The next morning, I told myself that I must go to Ghobrial. I had wronged him and hurt his feelings. I had spoken to him harshly, in a manner that did not respect his age as an elderly man and did not befit the love between us. I felt deep regret, especially since he had left the church hurt. I resolved to visit him, apologize, and ask for forgiveness.

I went to his house and knocked on the door. When he opened the door and saw me, he knelt down suddenly, casting himself down prostrate before me. I threw myself on the ground, kissing him and asking him to forgive me. He wept and said, "I have sinned!" How small I felt before the greatness of his heart!

He said, "Father, you come to me? I who could dare ask to make a speech! I should not have recommended myself. I raised my voice in church and did not obey. I was wrong, and you come to me?"

We spent that day in pure love, reading the Holy Bible and praying the psalms together. Then, deeply humbled and ashamed of what I had done, I went away, admiring this kind-hearted man who met my wrongdoing with kindness and blamed himself instead.

Years passed, during which this good man lived in the fear of God. Then, illness struck; he was diagnosed with kidney failure. His condition worsened, and, soon, he slipped into a coma. He was unconscious and completely unresponsive for three days, with no speech or eye movement.

It was the first day of Jonah's Fast when I heard about his critical condition. I hurried to visit him and give him the Eucharist. I was deeply moved because this man was dear to me. I loved him as my father; I loved his kind heart and his zealous, Christ-worshipping spirit.

I entered his hospital room, where he lay surrounded by his family, and something amazing happened. He opened his eyes and said, "'Blessed is he who comes in the name of the Lord!' [Ps 118:26]. Bring a chair for

Abouna to rest.[18] Welcome, *Abouna*!"

My heart rejoiced to see the light of God's grace shining in his face. I gave him the Holy Communion, prayed, and dismissed the angel of the offering.

Then, as I stood beside his bed, he began to speak strange and wondrous words: "What is this? A great celebration? All this—for me? No, I am not worthy. Who's that? David the Prophet, Job the Righteous, and our father Abraham? How wonderful! Who is carrying the chairs and arranging them? You, *Abouna* Bishoy? Impossible! No, Father, I am not worthy of all this...No, no—it's too much."

A few seconds later, his kind spirit departed to enjoy this joyous celebration prepared by the saints who would receive him. Yes, he saw the saints with his own eyes, and, in humility, cried out, "I am not worthy!"

Indeed, this is the spirit of the righteous at the moment of departure. As the spirit is leaving the body, the body is already frail and beginning to decay. In that state, the spiritual eyes and ears are no longer hindered by the limitations of the flesh; they can see and hear through the torn and fading body. So, Paradise may be revealed to the departing spirit.

The spirit sees and hears with the inner senses given

18 *Abouna* (أبونا) means "our father" in Arabic and is a title for a priest or monk.

by Christ, not with the eyes and ears of the flesh. Truly, blessed are the eyes that see and the ears that hear (Mt 13:16) and "Blessed are the dead who die in the Lord" (Rev 14:13).

✣

CHAPTER TWENTY

A Model Christian Family

"Behold, how good and how pleasant it is For brethren to dwell together in unity! It is like the precious oil upon the head, Running down on the beard, The beard of Aaron" (Ps 133:1–2). So spoke the Holy Spirit through the psalmist, praising Christian love. When brothers dwell together in spiritual love, they are like precious oil upon the head of Christ, running down to the hem of His garments, anointing both elders and youth each day and harmonizing them like the strings of a harp, as we say in the Church's morning prayers (Matins).

The Church has lived the profound experience of powerful, sincere love through the generations, uniting its members as one body and binding them together with divine compassion. Love, as Fr. Bishoy Kamel described it, is the lifeblood of the Church. We witnessed a blessed example of this in a family that began attending our church in Sporting in 1959, when it was founded. One of the homes of this family was adjacent to the church, and many of its members lived within the church's pastoral area, making them foundational stones of the church community. At the time, this family had over 50 members, many of whom were closely related, with most of their marriages occurring between cousins. Over the years, the Lord's blessings multiplied in every aspect of their lives, and, as their numbers grew, they continued to preserve their bond of love.

Every Sunday, the entire family—men, women, young, and old—would gather in one of their homes to pray together. They sang hymns and praises, recited psalms, read passages from the Holy Bible, and shared a meal of fellowship.

Unlike many other families, who often allow gossip, rivalry, and division to creep into their social gatherings, this blessed family maintained a spirit of unity. Negative traits often seen in family circles, like rumors, backbiting, jealousy, and judgment, were noticeably absent. Instead, this family overflowed with the sweet fruits of love; they were a true model of the Christian life.

Roots

To understand the origins of this beautiful phenomenon, which we hope to see spread throughout our church communities, we must look back to the roots of this spiritual love. It traces back to the elder mothers of the family, sisters by blood who grew up together in a village of Upper Egypt. From their childhood, they were nurtured by a living faith, untainted by philosophical reasoning, for theirs was not an age of intellectualism, but of piety, virtue, holiness, and the childlike simplicity of early believers. When they later moved to Cairo and eventually settled in Alexandria, they carried with them the leaven of faith and the depth of church life, including the fasting and prayers they had known since childhood. They planted this love for Christ in the hearts of their children and passed on the legacy of authentic Christianity to the next generation. How much the Church today needs such mothers!

One of these elderly mothers, known as Om Nazmy, lived in the house adjacent to the church. She was a truly devout woman, living a life of simplicity, depth, and love. Her heart was humble and wide, always open to others. She faced many trials in her life, including being widowed at a young age, but the hand of the Almighty always upheld her. She lived with her eldest son, his wife, and their children, along with her two other sons and one daughter. She also permanenetly housed a distant relative—an eldery man—not just because she had a large house, but because she had a large, love-filled heart.

Her youngest son graduated from medical school and worked for some time as a military physician, but he had always had a deep inclination toward solitude and spirtual devotion. He was loved by all—young and old, family and strangers alike. The Lord had filled him with abundant grace, and he often sought spiritual retreats in the holy monasteries. He formed deep friendships with some of the consecrated monks, including the late Bishop Arsenius of El-Minya, and often spent nights in prayer and periods of seclusion with them.

When his heart was fully at peace with the monastic calling, he decided to leave the world behind. One day, he returned home with one of the monks from the Monastery of St. Macarius the Great, the monastery where he intended to take his vows, and spoke with his mother about his decision. He asked for her blessing as he prepared to dedicate his life to God.

What a beautiful image of a righteous mother filled with the Spirit of God: she placed her hands on her son's head, blessed him, and prayed that the Lord would strengthen his path and complete his salvation. Her eyes were filled with tears, but her heart overflowed with the joy of offering her son as a pure sacrifice to Christ. Such mothers are rare to find today—those who willingly offer their children to the Church, giving their sons and daughters to Christ as holy offerings and encouraging them on the path of dedication to holiness, with full satisfaction and without selfishness or regret.

The Departure of the Righteous

After completing her good fight, this blessed mother

fell ill for a short time and then departed to the Lord in peace. Her face shone like that of an angel. Truly, "Precious in the sight of the Lord Is the death of His saints" (Ps 116:15). On the day of her departure, a Wednesday, her children, grandchildren, and loved ones gathered around her in the peace and serenity of prayer. Her only brother, Cantor Labib of St. Mina Church in Fleming, Alexandria, had been attending the Divine Liturgy.[19] When he arrived to the house afterward and was told of his sister's passing, he removed his *tarboosh* (traditional head covering), bowed his head before the priests, and said, "Pray for me. I have just received Holy Communion, and so I do not want to become upset." He continued to pray, raising his heart to Christ, and sought the intercessions of the Virgin Mary and St. Mina, so that his faith might not weaken. His behavior on that day was a powerful lesson to all who witnessed it, teaching them not to mourn as those without hope (1 Thess 4:13).

A Solemn Procession

The farewell procession for Om Nazmy was truly dignified. Her second son, a senior officer in the navy and a professor at the naval academy, was widely respected

19 The cantor is the deacon tasked with leading the chanters and congregation in prayers and praises. He is also tasked with teaching the hymns of the Church to the congregation. This person has to have graduated from St. Didymus Institute for Cantors.

and loved by all who knew him. In recognition of his mother's deep faith and the simple yet profound life she had led, military and naval units were dispatched to honor her with a full military procession. It was a fitting tribute to a woman who had lived a life of quiet strength and deep spirituality. Those who witnessed this remarkable scene marveled at the honor shown to this humble woman, remembering the words of our Lord: "Far be it from Me; for those who honor Me I will honor, and those who despise Me shall be lightly esteemed" (1 Sam 2:30).

The Cantor Labib

Om Nazmy's brother, Cantor Labib, was a pillar of ecclesiastical tradition in his generation. He possessed a profound knowledge of the Church's rites and was a master of Coptic hymnology, which he had studied from a young age. With great faithfulness, he passed these sacred hymns on to bishops, monks, priests, and deacons. He was unwavering in his commitment to the precise observance of the Church's liturgical traditions, teaching their deeper spiritual meanings to all who would listen and never altering or adding to them.

Those who lived alongside him saw a unique example of a true church cantor. Every time he served at the altar, he participated in the Holy Communion, never once standing before the Lord's table without being fully prepared to partake of the Holy Mysteries.[20] Like a priest who would never serve the Divine Liturgy without receiving Communion, Cantor Labib never approached the sacred altar without first purifying his heart and mind. For him, the Eucharist was the joy of life, the delight of his heart, and the source of his spiritual strength.

On His Deathbed

Cantor Labib reached a good old age, and, when his health became weak, he was taken to the Coptic Hospital, which contains a small church. He almost went into a coma.

One morning, he asked, "What's today?" and those around told him it was Wednesday. He then said, "Tell the priest to bring me the Holy Communion."

They answered, "We already told him, and he will give you Communion."

After a while, he opened his eyes and asked, "Where is the priest?"

They said, "The Holy Liturgy has not ended."

"He is very late."

---

20 The "Lord's table" refers to the altar where the bread and wine are placed and become the true Body and Blood of Christ. St. Paul refers to this when he says, "you cannot partake of the Lord's table and of the table of demons" (1 Cor 10:21).

They responded, "He will bring the Eucharist after the liturgy ends."

He asked the same question again. They gave him the same answer and said, "Be patient, Mr. Labib."

After a while, they heard him say what is recited before Communion: "Blessed is he who comes in the name of the Lord!" (Ps 118:26). He then seemed to be eating something. Then, he said the prayer recited after Holy Communion.

They woke him up, saying, "Here is the priest; he has brought you the Holy Communion."

But he said, "Father, I have taken Communion, thank God." They thought he was delirious, but he said, "Believe me, Father, Pope Kyrillos came here now and gave me the Holy Communion. I drank water after, and the taste of the Holy Communion is still in my mouth."

All those present were astonished and were sure what he said was true. They glorified God, who does great deeds through His saints. A short time after, this righteous man reposed in peace in the Lord.

After he departed, his family was bewildered by an amazing sight. When they opened his bedroom window, a dove entered his room, briefly stood on his bed, and then stood on his wardrobe from morning till evening. The dove would do this every day, as they tried in vain to take hold of it and drive it out. After 40 days, the dove disappeared.

The Lady Om Adly

The eldest sister of Om Nazmy and Cantor Labib, Om Adly, was wonderful in her profound prayers and faith. She taught her children a pious lifestyle and always told them to pray the psalms in the morning. Tribulations had no power over her or her children. Her eldest son, who was the CEO of a big firm, always said to me, "My mother taught me to pray. If I do not pray the psalms in the morning, the devil keeps jumping around me all day." As he acquired a life of piety, meekness, and love through the teachings of his mother, the Lord rendered his way to success. He was loved by all and continuously promoted. At any agency or administration he worked at, he preached love and peace among the people. If, at some place, something went wrong and quarrels ensued, they would send for Mr. Adly. As soon as he would come, peace would replace antagonism. How lovely is the practical Christian life!

All those who knew Om Adly testified to the fact that she had never contended with or been angry with anyone all her life. She would do good to everybody, and she would not forget the poor—she gave to them generously and lovingly, especially the peddlers, to whom she insisted on giving food when they knocked at her door. During the month of *Koiahk* in 1967, she became sick.[21] Her children and grandchildren gathered around her, singing praises and hymns and praying the psalms. I was beside her bed as they sang, and she said, "Children, is this not the month of *Koiahk*? Sing one of the *Koiahk* praises." As they were singing the praise, she gave up her spirit and entered into the eternal praises—life in the joy of the righteous.

21 *Koiahk* is the fourth month of the Coptic calendar. It falls during the Nativity Fast and is marked by additional melodies in the Midnight Praises. These beloved praises begin in the evening and often extend into the early morning, filling churches with children, adults, and elders who praise with all their hearts, anticipating the Savior's birth at the fast's end and glorifying His mother, St. Mary, who was worthy to carry Him in her womb for nine months.

CONCLUSION

Dear reader,

We have come to the conclusion of this small book, which contains a number of true stories of faith. May these stories focus your attention on the Rock of Ages, "Jesus, the author and finisher of our faith, who for the joy that was set before Him endured the cross, despising the shame" (Heb 12:2). May these stories also arouse in you spiritual perseverance and steadfastness in the confirmation of the hope that is in you.

Though the life of holiness, faith, and obedience to the commandments of our Lord Jesus Christ may indeed be a difficult road with a narrow gate (Mt 7:14), it is by no means impossible. By the grace of Christ, it is entirely possible. We deduce from these real stories the words of St. Paul the Apostle: "I can do all things through Christ who strengthens me" (Phil 4:13). I know that what is impossible with men is possible with God (Lk 18:27), or, as the Lord said, "all things are possible to him who believes" (Mk 9:23).

Therefore, fight the good fight and hold fast to the eternal life that you have been called to (1 Tim 6:12). May this small book be a source of blessing and salvation for many. Amen.

www.ingramcontent.com/pod-product-compliance
Ingram Content Group UK Ltd.
Pitfield, Milton Keynes, MK11 3LW, UK
UKHW040021200726
13854UKWH00001B/297

9 798894 830230